What people are ~~~~~ ~~
WHY IS MY B.   RD

This is an interesting approac~~~~~~~ ~~~~~ ~~
with one of the most disturbin~~~~~~ ~~~~~ ~~~ occur with
new babies—the fussy period at the end of the day. A
reliable interpretation of the small baby's cries, shared
with an understanding pediatrician, can certainly help
to reduce the new parent's natural anxiety.

T. Berry Brazelton, M.D.
Professor Emeritus, Pediatrics
Harvard Medical School
Author of TOUCHPOINTS

Bruce Taubman's common-sense approach works.
Backed up by research, his easy-to-follow program will
help you understand why your baby cries and what you
can do about it. You and your child will be happier as a
result.

Steven M. Altschuler, M.D.
Physician-in-Chief
Children's Hospital of Philadelphia

...the flow charts and the general tips in the book have
proved invaluable to us. When the baby is unsettled, we
just go through the routine....Your book does make
perfect sense. I plan to give copies as shower gifts in the
future!

Mari Corson, new mother

WHY IS MY BABY CRYING?

DISCARD

The 7-Minute Program for Soothing the Fussy Baby

Bruce Taubman, M.D.

White Hat Communications

Harrisburg, Pennsylvania

Why Is My Baby Crying?
The 7-Minute Program
for Soothing the Fussy Baby

by Bruce Taubman, M.D.

Published by:

White *Hat Communications*

P.O. Box 5390
Harrisburg, PA 17110-0390
717-238-3787 (voice)
717-238-2090 (fax)

ISBN: 1-929109-00-8
Library of Congress Catalog Card Number: 00-131082

Note: Names and identities of patients and their families have been changed to protect their privacy.

In memory of John A. Askin, M.D.

Acknowledgment

I would like to thank Suzanne Lipsett for her help in writing and editing this book.

Note to the Reader

This book covers all aspects of crying in healthy infants. Here you will learn why your baby cries, what those cries mean, and what scientific researchers have determined about the function of crying in your baby's growth and development process. Further, you will learn how to respond to your baby's cries within seven minutes, under every possible circumstance. The book presents an easy-to-follow method for the quick cure and effective prevention of colic, but the information applies to all infants, not just those with colic. Whether your baby cries a lot or a little, this book will answer many questions about those first, often baffling three months, when you and your baby are getting to know each other and the groundwork is being laid for a lifelong relationship.

Note from the Publisher

I first read Bruce Taubman's *WHY IS MY BABY CRY-ING* in 1992 as a new mother. My son was only a few months old, and in my "spare time," I read every book I could find that would tell me what his behaviors meant, how they compared to the "norm," and what my husband and I could do to be the best parents possible.

WHY IS MY BABY CRYING is one of the books that stood out in my mind as I read all the "baby parenting" books that were available. It was easy to read, made sense, had a clear focus, and was helpful. I have always believed that children should be listened to and taken seriously, and Dr. Taubman extends this belief to the earliest days of an infant's life. His approach encourages parents to listen to their children, even as tiny infants, and to try to determine what they are "saying," even when they can communicate only with cries.

I believe this is one of the most important lessons parents can learn—to listen to their children. In addition, Bruce Taubman's method of responding to a baby's cries is easy to follow and it will help many babies and parents spend more quiet, enjoyable time with each other.

I read *WHY IS MY BABY CRYING* again in the past year, this time with my "publisher's hat" on. The book was out of print, and I was glad to have the opportunity to work with Dr. Taubman to make it available to parents again. He is a caring pediatrician who has helped many parents respond to the needs of their fussy babies. He wants more parents to have the chance to use the methods he has used with his own patients, and that is why he wrote this book.

WHY IS MY BABY CRYING gave me answers I couldn't get anywhere else. If you find it as useful as I did as a new mother, my goal as publisher of this book will have been accomplished.

Linda M. Grobman

Table of Contents

Chapter 1
"I Had No Idea": What Colic Can Do to Families

A TYPICAL CASE

"I had no idea parenthood could be as tough as this," Margie told me in a choked voice. She looked pale and drawn, and I watched her struggle to keep her composure as Steven, her two-month-old infant, wriggled and fussed on her lap. Her husband, Tom, occasionally reached over to pat the boy on the stomach, but he too looked strained.

The fact was the two parents were exhausted. They had been taking turns staying up with Steven for hours every night. After walking the baby around the dark house and finally turning in, they would again be awakened by the child's crying and the pattern would be repeated. The pediatrician they had been seeing had reassured them that Steven was perfectly healthy—"just a little colicky, that's all." There was nothing to be done, he said, but to hang in there until Steven passed the three-month mark. Make sure he's comfortable, do what you can to endure the commotion, and look forward to getting some pleasure out of parenting when the colic lifts.

Margie and Tim had endured it for a while, but after the first month, they became assertive and insisted their pediatrician give some active treatment. Margie's mother felt that the baby was suffering from gas pains, so the couple raised the question with Steven's doctor. He prescribed a medicine to treat gas (a prescription designed for adults, since there is no treatment for abdominal gas in infants).

A month later, with the medicine having had no apparent effect on Steven's nighttime crying, the exasperated couple came to me. It didn't take much to gain their confidence. I simply told them what I had learned from years of working with colicky babies, that infant colic syndrome is a reality and a problem—but it is a *treatable* and *preventable* problem, not one simply to be endured until it goes away. After examining Steven carefully and finding him to be a sound, healthy, steadily growing youngster, I turned to his parents.

As with most situations affecting infants, infant colic syndrome is a family condition, involving everyone who lives in the household. Because it affects the family's sleep and because if unattended it can go on for months, infant colic syndrome can turn a family upside down and disrupt those first weeks in which parents and child get to know each other and establish their patterns of interaction. With the baby crying, the night's restfulness shattered, daily business fragmented by exhaustion, and seemingly everyone offering advice, parents of colicky babies need a chance to sort things out and gain a clear perspective of their situation. As a first step in treatment, I encouraged Margie and Tim to take the time they needed to do just that.

Tim and Margie had worked hard to have Steven and had suffered a number of disappointments in their efforts to start a family. Margie had had two first-trimester miscarriages and one difficult second-trimester one. They and their obstetrician were starting to wonder whether full-term pregnancy was possible for them when Margie became pregnant once more. This pregnancy ran a perfectly normal course with no problems, and by the eighth month, Margie and Tim had allowed themselves to become very excited about parenthood. They spent every weekend working on the nursery and layette. The couple's small business, which they conducted from a home office, was going well, and they decided they could afford Margie's absence for a year so she could devote herself to their baby full time. The last month of pregnancy was a happy time of anticipation for them both. They knew that by becoming parents, they were making a major lifestyle change, and they were looking forward to the shift with pleasure. How different things would be, and how delightful the novelty!

How different indeed. Margie woke up in labor at about eleven one night and, with Tim coaching, delivered Steven at noon the next day. "And we haven't caught up on our sleep since," they said, nearly in unison. From Steven's birth onward, he was up every night crying for hours and passing gas. In the first two weeks of life, he woke every three hours to nurse, and he was a fussy feeder, so each nursing session took a lot of time and attention. In Steven's third week, he began waking at night more and more often, crying and passing gas. The problem became steadily worse, with crying sessions in the evenings extending into the night.

Tim's mother was of the old school. "Once the baby's been fed, let a crying child cry. It's good for the character and good for the lungs." But neither Tim nor Margie believed in that approach. They did everything they could think of to stop their child's crying. The discouragement they felt when Steven didn't respond turned into disappointment and then despair. They had had such plans for their baby. They had felt so ready and willing to give completely of themselves to make their deeply wanted child happy. And through all their attempts—at walking him, bringing in the stroller and strolling him around the house, taking him out for car rides at three in the morning, even walking through town at that hour with an inconsolable Steven crying in a baby carrier on Tim's chest—the baby remained unresponsive and clearly miserable.

Tim was becoming frantic about his work. He was exhausted when he sat down at his desk in the morning, and unable to concentrate during the day when Steven's cries filtered through the walls. His pleas to Margie to keep the baby quiet ended in terrible arguments. And Margie herself felt like a complete failure as a mother. "If I can't console a two-month-old, what kind of a mother am I going to make? I always thought that love was enough—that if you loved your baby, all you had to do to make him happy was, well, to love him. Now I'm not sure *what's* required. Maybe I just don't love Steven enough, after all. I never knew it could be this tough. I never expected to be…"

I had to urge her to complete her sentence.

"…disappointed."

She had every right to feel disappointed and unhappy, I reassured her. And her reactions were in no way unusual. Crying is meant to alarm parents; that's exactly what it's for. A baby's cry is the signal that an action needs to be taken. But the question is, what action? In the case of Steven, the atmosphere had grown so frantic and the parents so tired and distraught that answering that question had become impossible. Confusion and noise were generating chaos in the house. Margie and Tim's self-blame, frustration, and regret at having had Steven at all were understandable—but also added fuel to the situation. It was my task to help this couple see that their own disappointment, sleep deprivation, and emotional turmoil were important components of the infant colic syndrome.

But there were also conflicting opinions and prescriptions that Margie and Tim's own parents were offering that needed to be taken into account. Both sets of grandparents were strong-minded people, and both had strong ideas about what was going on with their first grandchild.

Margie's mother was absolutely convinced that Steven's crying showed he was in pain, and she blamed the pain on Margie's diet. She didn't' approve of breast-feeding in the first place, considering it old fashioned, but felt that since Margie insisted, she should be restricting her own food intake to bland, high-protein foods such as dairy products and unseasoned meats. Both she and her husband watched Margie's food consumption like hawks whenever they had the chance. To Margie, they seemed to be treating her as a young girl again, just when her own self-esteem was suffering, and more than once she had given in to the temptation to hand Steven over to their seemingly more experienced and self-confident care.

Tim's father, on the other hand, aligned himself staunchly with Tim's mother and Steven's previous pediatrician. "Do nothing; babies cry. That's what they're all about," he said whenever he was around for one of Steven's crying episodes. "Leave him be," he advised. "He'll be fine once his nervous system matures." Whenever he was present and Steven began to fuss, Margie and Tim had to face his disapproval when they responded to and worried about the baby's cries.

What a mess! Margie and Tim had gone from the quiet expectancy of late pregnancy to a chaos of conflict and nerve-wracking noise. In a fog of exhaustion, they had come to wonder how they would ever make it through the eighteen or so years of Steven's development if the first two months were proving to be so daunting. What was happening to them, and how could they stop it?

TAKING CARE OF THE CARE-GIVERS: BEGINNING WITH YOURSELF

It may surprise you to see that this book opens not with a section on the symptoms of colic but on the parents' predicament. In starting this way, I have two deliberate goals in mind: to acknowledge and describe some of the aspects of colic that often get overlooked but that quickly become important components of the problem and need to be treated, and to address the psychological matters that are frequently ignored. Colic is treatable and preventable in infants, but expecting yourself to carry out a careful plan of observation and treatment when you are frazzled, anxious, exhausted, confused, and afraid you are doing the wrong thing is simply too much. Therefore, as I did with Margie and Tim, I encourage you to step back—just for a moment—from the puzzle of your healthy child's cries and gain a new perspective of your situation.

If your newborn has been pronounced healthy by a pediatrician but has been crying inconsolably for a number of weeks, the following points, to a greater or lesser degree, should sound familiar:

•*Anxiety over your child's well being.* The cry of a child is designed to evoke anxious concern. Its pitch and timbre mean "Help me!" Mothers prevented from tending to their crying babies exhibit a wide range of physiological changes associated with anxiety and even fear—their heartbeats speed up, they perspire and experience shakiness in their limbs, and their alertness increases. These symptoms are related to an increase in adrenaline, which primes the body for action. When that action is frustrated, the symptoms remain, and are experienced as what we call anxiety. That same set of factors arises and remains—with the same result, anxiety—when parents take action but the baby's cries continue unabated.

Adding to this set of physiological anxiety symptoms is the parents' understandable and predictable fear that something in the assessment of the child's health has been overlooked. This might begin as a nagging subconscious concern that swells into outright panic as the crying—"Help me!"—continues over nights and weeks. What if my baby is in pain? What if there is something seriously wrong that the pediatrician missed?

•*The discomfort engendered by sleep deprivation and interrupted sleep.* Perhaps the most you can do in the circumstances is to remain aware that interrupted sleep and exhaustion result in a reduced ability to concentrate, slowed reaction times, irritability, and an all-around feeling of discomfort. Until your child's colic is cured, your sleep will suffer, but it is important to understand that the sleep loss itself is a factor in the problem.

•*Guilt and disappointment in your relationship with your infant.* Like Margie and Tim, you may have gone overnight from dreamy expectation to an overdose of reality in the form of your child's inconsolable crying. Give yourself the break you need. Understand that you would not be human if you did not feel disappointed at your frustrated expectations. For reasons unclear to you, your baby is unresponsive to your best efforts at meeting his or her needs. Take it from one who has heard the story many times: Disappointment and dismay are universal reactions among parents of inconsolable babies. You may not be able to eliminate the sting of these emotions, but knowing their pervasiveness may keep you from experiencing guilt at having them. With the help of this book and your own clarity of mind, be reassured that you will solve the problem of your baby's cries. At this point, simply allow yourself to feel what you feel.

•*Chaos and confusion in all aspects of your life.* The first weeks of your baby's life are critical in terms of adaptation. Your whole family is shifting. If you have other children, each one is making a complex psychological adjustment to the presence of the baby and to the shifts in your attention and priorities. If this is your first baby, you are making perhaps an even more massive adjustment as the focus of your attention shifts from yourself and your mate to your baby, perhaps for the first time in your lives.

Compound this complexity of adjustment with large doses of inconsolable crying, and you are faced with a period of tremendous stress. Stress, like sleep deprivation, can wreck your focus on life. It can push you off your stride in dealing with your daily responsibilities by drawing constant attention to your own needs for calm. Again, the antidote is acknowledging and understanding the dynamics of the situation. By recognizing that your situation is indeed highly stressful, you can allow yourself to tend to inner needs that you might otherwise be tempted to ignore. In this crucial period of adjustment, try to use the stress-reducing methods that have worked for you in the past.

By taking care of yourself, you can keep yourself from reaching the point of one desperate mother whose telephone call I returned:

"Oh, Dr. Taubman, thank heavens it's you," she said in a shaky voice over the cries of the two-month-old Alice. "I was just sitting here with the telephone book open to the A's."

"The A's?" I asked.

"For adoption agencies. I've come to the end of my rope."

There's a practical reason for starting this book with concern for your own well being, of course. Without you in control, who will be? With the whole household succumbing to the anxiety and chaos an inconsolable crier can create, who's going to solve the problem? So take deep breaths, take long walks with your baby, take turns with the baby if you have a spouse, and be sure to take naps when your baby finally drops off to sleep. Most of all, take comfort in the fact that help is on the way. Once you read this book and put the program described in Chapter 5 into action, your baby's crying will be under control within seven days.

Chapter 2

"But Our Pediatrician Said": What Infant Colic Is Not

WHAT IS COLIC?

If you ask parents to define infant colic, they almost always answer that it involves pain, usually abdominal pain. But when a physician diagnoses a child as having *infant colic*—or the *infant colic syndrome,* which is the term I prefer to use—he or she is talking about a baby with the following characteristics: young, usually under four months of age, and perfectly healthy in all respects. The child is gaining weight steadily and growing normally and a physical examination shows the baby to be entirely normal. Despite all this, however, the baby has episodes of excessive, inconsolable crying—that is, the baby cries at certain times throughout the day and the parents are unable to stop it, regardless of what they do.

When we call such a baby healthy, we mean that he or she has no signs of illness such as coughing, runny nose, fever, rash, vomiting, diarrhea, or constipation. The only symptom other than crying that such a baby might have is gas; infants with infant colic syndrome often pass a great deal of gas during their crying episodes.

9

Essentially then, *infant colic syndrome* refers to a healthy infant who cries a great deal for no apparent reason—period. You will notice that in this definition, there is no mention whatsoever of abdominal pain. In drawing attention to this fact, I come to the crux of a long-standing controversy.

Many physicians believe that infant colic syndrome has nothing to do with abdominal pain at all. Nevertheless, in the minds of many others, and in the general public outside the medical community, the term *colic* remains stubbornly linked with the notion of pain.

In the 1930s and 1940s, physicians first began to look closely at babies who cried inconsolably, studying the manner of their crying very intently. They found that the babies drew up their legs, hardened their abdomens, turned red, and passed gas as they cried. There is no question that the infants *looked* as if they were in pain. In fact, the observing physicians concluded that they were having abdominal cramps, and the parents usually agreed wholeheartedly with this observation. Intuitively, the parents believed their babies were experiencing cramps as well, so, appropriately enough, they referred to the condition as "colic."

For the next twenty to thirty years, doctors treated infant colic syndrome on the assumption that the cause was abdominal pain. They prescribed various medications aimed at treating abdominal cramps, but in fact saw very little relief as a result. In thinking about the cause of the supposed pain, doctors usually agreed that it was gas, since these babies generally passed a great deal of gas during their crying episodes. However, no one could explain why some babies had more gas than others and why gas seemed to be more problematic for some than for others. They looked at feeding techniques, at composition of the infants' and mothers' diets, at the possibility that colicky babies digested the sugar in milk poorly—but could collect no evidence to support the proposed theories.

Despite the lack of evidence that gas pains cause colic, many doctors to this day still subscribe to the theory. And many of these prescribe a medication used in adults for excessive stomach gas, though there is no proof that it helps.

Other doctors who concluded from the evidence that gas was not the culprit in colic then turned their attention to infant—and maternal—diet. In fact, in the 1960s, food allergies came into vogue as the explanation for a good many then-unexplained human ailments. During this time, some doctors proposed that an allergy to cow's milk caused abdominal pain, which in turn caused colic, and they recommended formula changes for bottle-fed babies with colic.

In the early 1970s, with colic as persistent as ever in the infant population, more and more doctors began to realize that treating this condition on the assumption that it was caused by abdominal pain simply wasn't working. Once again, attention focused on the crying itself: What was its nature? What could it tell us? In this phase, doctors realized that *all* babies who have been crying for more than a few minutes—*regardless of the cause*—cry in the same manner. *All* crying babies:

- Draw up their legs

- Harden their abdomens

- Turn red

- Often pass gas

Babies whose reasons for crying are known cry this way, and so do babies whose reasons are unknown. For example, a baby whose leg is irritated by a DPT (diphtheria pertussis tetanus) injection will show the signs I have just listed; so will a baby who has been frightened by a loud noise or a baby whose feeding is long overdue and is hungry.

The important conclusion, then, is that you simply can't tell by observing a baby why he is crying. For that matter, abdominal pain *always* appears to be the cause, whether DPT or hunger is the culprit or some unknown demon is making the baby cry.

Slowly, given this generally agreed-on observation, many physicians came to accept the notion that episodes of inconsolable crying were not related to abdominal pain. The term *infant colic* is now understood in medical circles to refer to the crying episodes alone—with no reference to pain or its causes. It is easy to understand, however, why so many lay people—and doctors, too—still associate inconsolable crying with abdominal pain despite the evidence to the contrary.

The next section examines our current, most common theories about the causes of colic. You'll notice another fact about medical knowledge as you read it: *Old theories die hard.* Many of the theories to which doctors still commonly subscribe are the very ones our survey showed to be incorrect, unsubstantiated by evidence.

First, though, let me return to the question that began this chapter and reiterate its answer: What is infant colic syndrome? *Infant colic syndrome is simply excessive inconsolable crying in healthy infants for no readily apparent reason.*

One qualification is necessary to make this simple definition perfectly clear—a definition of the phrase "excessive crying." How much crying is excessive crying? The normal range of crying for a four- to six-week-old infant is *thirty to ninety minutes per twenty-four hours,* so crying over that amount is considered excessive. (This range refers to the actual crying time as recorded by parents in highly-detailed records kept in "crying journals"; it does not include breaks in between.) Infant crying decreases after six weeks of age.

Your baby has infant colic syndrome if he or she:

- Is under four months of age (note that this refutes a widespread myth that colic disappears by the age of three months)

- Is perfectly healthy, with no vomiting or diarrhea
- Has episodes of inconsolable crying
- Cries for more than ninety minutes a day.

MYTHS SURROUNDING INFANT COLIC SYNDROME AND ITS TREATMENT

Our short historical overview made it clear that erroneous attitudes and theories have a way of lingering over years and sometimes decades, even within medical circles. The fact is, bad advice, both from medical and lay sources, is the norm where infant colic syndrome is concerned. And too often, inaccurate information interferes with the fundamental requirement for the treatment program described in this book: the parents' ability to observe with clarity and precision. Given the intense desire parents have to solve the mystery of their infant's colic, it is not unusual for their interpretations of their observations to be influenced by the advice they receive both from doctors and well-meaning friends and relatives. To help you safeguard against the common myths and errors surrounding colic, I will cover these various approaches in some detail. Remember, the information in the list that follows is *incorrect* and has the potential to lead you *away* from the solution of your baby's colic problem.

Myth 1: *Infant colic syndrome is caused by the infant's allergy to the commercial formula.*

Whenever a colicky infant is feeding on formula, someone—either a doctor or a lay person—is bound to suggest that the infant is allergic to the formula and is experiencing abdominal pain as a result. What evidence is there to support this theory? A study that appeared in the pediatric literature in 1982 showed that 71 percent of infants benefit from a formula change, but this study was itself flawed in its design, and its conclusion was therefore incorrect.[1]

The major flaw in the study was that in the group of infants studied, the researchers included some with gastrointestinal symptoms *other* than gas, specifically vomiting and diarrhea. But the one factor about colic that is universally accepted is that it is an affliction of otherwise healthy babies.

Vomiting and diarrhea are symptoms of a variety of medical problems, but not colic. If your baby cries excessively and has vomiting and/or diarrhea, he or she does not have infant colic syndrome. Given those symptoms, your baby's doctor should be aggressively seeking their cause.

Milk allergy is, indeed, one of the most common causes of diarrhea and/or vomiting in infants who cry excessively, and for these babies a formula change would be the correct treatment. No infants with vomiting or diarrhea were asked to participate in my studies on the infant colic syndrome, and I found absolutely no instances of formula allergy. These studies showed that for the baby with infant colic syndrome, changing formula is a waste of time. You can prove this yourself easily enough with a single formula change.

Mr. and Mrs. Kinney came to see me with their five-week-old infant, Jon, because, they said, he was·having abdominal cramps. They were positive that the problem was his formula and insisted that I recommend a different one. Their former pediatrician had already changed Jon's formula a number of times and had tried to convince them simply to wait out the crying until, said the doctor (erroneously), "his nervous system matures."

---

1. L. Lothe, T. Lindberg, and I. Jakobsson, "Cow Milk Formula as a Cause of Infantile Colic: A Double-Blind Study," *Pediatrics* 70 (1982): 7-10.

Jon was a healthy baby with good weight gain and no diarrhea or vomiting. I was convinced that a formula change would only put us off the track, but the Kinneys were adamant. They wanted the formula changed, and Jon's progress under the change monitored. I agreed on the condition that if nothing changed, they would try the treatment approach described later in this book. Agreed, they said.

I put Jon on Nutramigen, a hypoallergenic formula that contains only hydrolyzed protein. By virtue of the molecular structure of this substance, it is physically impossible to be allergic to it. True to my expectations, nothing about Jon's crying pattern changed. The Kinneys agreed to try a different approach, but they had not given up their preconceptions easily. They had been pinning their hopes on this solution, and felt frustrated and over-whelmed when it didn't work.

The Kinneys' strong adherence to one of the colic myths is not at all unusual. Not only are the myths familiar, they are stubborn, as you yourself will discover when you try to refute them in others. And they often function to hold the chaos and confusion at bay. For some parents, not until all the old "solutions" fail does the emotional reality of their child's inconsolable distress hit home.

One more point is important here: Your colicky baby might improve with a formula change, but only by coincidence. Many babies with colic do get better without specific treatment, and this spontaneous improvement can happen as easily while you are experimenting with formula as at any other time. If you try a formula change and your baby improves, I strongly recommend that, as a test of your observations, you return to using the original formula and note whether the crying returns. (Nutramigen is quite expensive, and you'll not want to be using it if it is unnecessary.)

Myth 2: *Colic in breast-fed babies is caused by something in the mother's diet.*

It has been found that in nursing mothers who drink cow's milk, a small amount of the protein in cow's milk shows up in the breast milk. Physicians who believe that infant colic syndrome is caused by cow's milk protein allergy point to this as the source of the problem in colicky infants who are breast-fed. These doctors treat infant colic syndrome by putting the mothers on a milk-free diet. Three studies in the pediatric literature have measured the effectiveness of this approach. One study showed no benefit whatsoever.[2] Two studies (by the same investigators) showed an improvement in 35 percent of the cases.[3] Again, however, these studies included babies with vomiting and diarrhea, rendering the results invalid as a measure of allergy in *healthy* babies. My own studies contradict the notion that restricting milk or any other substance in the mother's diet reduces crying in colicky infants.

Manipulating the diet of a nursing mother is not only of no benefit; it can be hazardous as well. I have known nursing mothers—like Margie, described in Chapter 1— who have restricted their diets to such a degree that they endangered their own nutrition. Successful breast-feeding depends on a well-nourished mother, and fooling around with the mother's diet can affect the nutrition of both baby and mother.

Caffeine, however, is an exception to my rule. I urge nursing mothers to eat what they wish but to eliminate

---

2. R. W. Evans, A. R. Allardyce, and D. M. Fergusson, Brent Taylor, "Maternal Diet and Infantile Colic in Breast-fed Infants," *Lancet* 1 (1981): 1340-1343.

3. I. Jakobsson and T. Lindberg, "Cow's Milk as a Cause of Infantile Colic in Breast-fed Infants," *Lancet* 11 (1978): 437-439; and "Cow's Milk Proteins Cause Infantile Colic in Breast-fed Infants: A Double-Blind Crossover Study," *Pediatrics* 71 (1983): 268-271.

caffeine from their diets. Caffeine consumed by nursing mothers does enter breast milk in very small amounts. Most physicians do not feel that this amount is large enough to harm the breast-feeding infant, but because some adults are very sensitive to the effects of this drug, I assume that some babies are, too. In a baby with a heightened sensitivity to caffeine, even a small amount of the substance might produce irritability.

Myth 3: *Gas causes infant colic syndrome.*

This is the familiar myth whose growth was traced earlier in the chapter. As I explained there, the theory is linked to the observation that many babies with colic pass a great deal of gas. This observation is accurate, but physicians who subscribe to the theory that gas is the cause are putting the cart before the horse. Babies with infant colic syndrome do not cry because they have gas; they have excessive gas because they cry so much.

One of the main sources of excessive gas is swallowed air. Babies who cry a great deal, for whatever reason, swallow a lot of air. Further, the action of increasing abdominal pressure will cause gas in the rectum to be passed. If you look at strenuously crying babies, you will see that they indeed increase the pressure on the abdomen by hardening it; as a result, gas is passed from the rectum.

Any baby who cries for a significant amount of time *for whatever reason* will therefore build up intestinal gas (by swallowing lots of air) and pass gas rectally (by increasing abdominal pressure). Clearly, it is the crying that causes the gas, not vice versa.

Myth 4: *Abdominal cramps cause infant colic syndrome.*

Some physicians believe that abdominal cramps cause colic, though they usually make no attempt to explain the source of such cramps. Often they are pragmatists more interested in using a medication that "works" than in determining underlying causes. This can be a dangerous approach, for it turns out that the single medicine shown to have an effect in relieving colic is one called dicyclomine hydrochloride, known more familiarly by its trade name, Bentyl. This medication is an antispasmodic intended for adults, and its side effects include drowsiness and lethargy. Physicians who prescribe it for colic do so on the assumption that it relieves the mysterious, undocumented abdominal cramps. It is just as possible, however—and is my own belief—that it is the side effects, not the antispasmodic effect, that reduce crying—by sedating the infant, or medicinally inducing sleep. Thus, the fact that Bentyl reduces colic in some excessively crying infants in no way confirms that these infants were suffering from abdominal cramps.

But this point is a technicality compared with the other consequences of the use of Bentyl in infants. In fact, no one knows how often these side effects occur when used in young infants or how intense they might be. Even more alarming, however, are the recent reports of serious, life-threatening side effects—differing from those showing up in adults—from the use of this drug in infants under three months of age. Episodes of apnea (interrupted breathing), seizures, coma, and even death have been reported with the use of Bentyl in this age group.

Clearly, the risks of using this drug for infants far outweigh any possible reductions in excessive crying. Fortunately, as you will read in the next chapter, infant colic syndrome can be treated and prevented effectively without the use of any medication whatsoever.

Myth 5: *The crying in colic is the result of immaturity of the nervous system.*

The premise of this theory is that the crying associated with infant colic syndrome results not from pain but from "nonspecific irritability," a kind of undefined distress. It argues that the nervous system is immature at birth and, as a result, is highly sensitive (to one degree or another, depending on the individual) to external stimuli. The colicky infant, then, is at the hypersensitive end of the spectrum and he or she cries as a reaction to continual nervous system stimulation. As the nervous system matures, the theory goes, the sensitivity and thus the crying recede.

This theory is the basis for the famous "hands-off" approach to excessively crying infants. Proponents believe that there is no specific treatment for colic except to wait it out. Further, they argue that the things parents *usually* do in the attempt to assuage their children's distress—holding, rocking, walking, talking, and so on—only increase the problem by adding to the stimuli assaulting the baby's immature nervous system. They recommend that the parents simply put down the inconsolably crying baby and walk away. In very extreme cases, some believers recommend sedation.

Many medical textbooks and scientific journals espouse this theory, and it has influenced the way a great many doctors throughout the country approach infant colic syndrome. They consider the problem to be harmless and self-limited—that is, one that the baby will outgrow naturally—and as a result, they do not take the problem very seriously. They see their proper role as reassurer of the parents, not treater of the infant, since, according to the theory, there is no treatment for colic except time.

Because these physicians sincerely believe in this theory, they are usually quite successful in making the parents feel better about their colicky infant—as long as the office visit lasts. At home, however, when an episode starts, very few parents are comfortable about leaving their babies to cry. Rather, they experience the intense irritation and anxiety of people primed for but prohibited from acting. Parents can stuff pillows around their heads, turn up the volume on the stereo, or run the shower, but wherever they are in the house, they'll be sweating it out, literally. Perspiration, shaky limbs, accelerated heartbeat and breathing, perhaps a sickish feeling, and certainly an acute, insuppressible alertness will assail them as they try to ignore their babies' cries of distress.

Still, many doctors subscribe to the immature-nervous-system theory. If your pediatrician takes this approach, there are some important questions that you as parents need to ask before you accept the theory as true.

Is there any hard evidence that this theory is true?

No. The hypersensitivity concept is only a hypothesis.

Has anyone shown that leaving colicky babies alone results in less crying than walking with them?

No. I studied this very question and found that, if there was a change, leaving crying babies alone resulted in more, not less, crying than does walking with them.

Is it true that all babies with infant colic syndrome get better within three months?

No. Many babies I have treated have all the characteristics of infant colic syndrome except that they are more than three months old.

Is it really harmless to let a crying baby cry?

No. The child may not suffer per se, but the failure to respond to infant cries can adversely affect the parent-infant attachment. In other words, an infant's cries are designed to be answered by the care-giver. Choosing not to respond is to impose an artificial—that is, unnatural—influence on the growing relationship between the infant and his or her care-givers. Because the fundamental work of the first months of a child's life is the forging of this very attachment, forcing artificial limitations on it can have serious negative results.

?Myth 6: *The crying of the baby with colic is from gastro-esophageal reflux.*

This is the latest fad in the long list of unproven explanations for the cause of infant colic. Gastro-esophageal reflux is a condition in which the stomach contents reflux back up the esophagus, the tube that carries food from the mouth to the stomach. In adults, once food has been swallowed, it is abnormal for it to regurgitate back up the esophagus toward the mouth. If this occurs on a chronic basis, it causes "heartburn." This is the term used to describe the pain adults experience with gastro-esophageal reflux.

However, gastro-esophageal reflux is not abnormal in infants. The system used by the body to prevent regurgitation of food from the stomach up the esophagus is quite sophisticated. It involves the coordination of the swallowing motion of the esophagus, which moves food into the stomach, and a circular band of muscle at the base of the esophagus that acts as a valve to prevent regurgitation of food. This system is immature in infants and does not work well. Hence, babies are "spitters." Think about it. Babies often spit up their feeds to one degree or another and we consider it normal. Yet spitting is actually regurgitation of food, a behavior that would be abnormal in an adult.

So. gastro-esophageal reflux, spitting, is quite common and normal in infants during the first several months of life. Unlike adults, infants seem protected from the painful effects of reflux. Some physicians have suggested that perhaps the infant with colic lacks this natural protection and is crying from heartburn. They recommend that colicky infants be treated with the same medication we use to treat adult heartburn, such as Zantac (ranitidine) and Propulsid (cisapride). I have several problems with the whole idea that colic could be caused by gastro-esophageal reflux and treating infants with these medications.

- Just as in the case of milk protein allergy causing colic (Myth 1), I think it is very unlikely that even if an infant does experience pain from gastro-esophageal reflux, the only symptom will be crying. I would expect these infants to be poor feeders, have weight loss, and/or have gross or microscopic blood in their feces or in the material they spit up. The reason I believe this is that adults with heartburn have inflammation of the esophagus. When the esophagus is inflamed, it often bleeds and eating is painful.

- Any medication can have adverse side effects, especially in young babies. Therefore, I never use medication to treat young infants unless I am sure of the diagnosis. For example, the drug Propulsid, used to prevent gastro-esophageal reflux, has been reported to cause abnormal heart rhythms and even death on rare occasion.

- No studies have been conducted to provide evidence that verifies this theory on the cause of colic. That is why there is a question mark next to Myth 6. Along with my colleagues at The Children's Hospital of Philadelphia, I am in the process of obtaining approval to perform a study to scientifically evaluate the influence of gastro-esophageal reflux on crying in the colicky baby.

I have explored the familiar myths surrounding colic, because they can lead you far afield in your efforts to calm your baby. You are now armed against the ·well-intended but often misguided advice you have heard (or will hear) concerning your child. Having covered in detail what *does not* cause infant colic, let's turn to see what *does.*

Chapter 3
Crying as Communication

This book and the colic cure it proposes are based on a revolutionary idea, that infant cries are communication—specific messages from infant to parent.

As Chapter 2 suggested, the accepted theories on the cause of colic take one of two approaches. One assumes that colicky infants cry because they are in pain. The other assumes that these cries are simply expressions of a generalized irritability. Until very recently, these theories have remained unchallenged. But now researchers are showing, and my own studies have indicated, that both these assumptions are wrong. My studies have shown that colicky babies are not in pain. And scientists now accept the fact that for babies in the first few months of life, crying is far from meaningless; rather, it is the infant's primary means of expressing and communicating basic needs.

Laying aside the question of pain for a detailed discussion of it later, what does this idea of infant communication tell us about the age-old mystery of colic? Colicky babies, like all other babies, cry to communicate specific messages to their parents. The fact that these babies appear to be inconsolable indicates that their messages are not getting through, at least not quickly enough. These babies with colic, who are often single-minded and tenacious individuals, soon become frustrated at the mis-communication. With frustration comes agitation, and at this point not even the accurate response to the baby's original message can quell the cries. Here, in a nutshell, is a basic outline of this new understanding of colic:

1. The baby cries, sending a specific message to the parent regarding a basic need.

2. The parent misinterprets the message and fails to meet the need signaled by the cry.

3. The baby's frustration leads to agitation so great that he or she is now unable to respond even when the parent makes the correct response to the original signal.

The baby's cry, then, is a message. The point is simple to grasp, but it challenges centuries of thinking. Babies' cries have always been considered irritating behavior to be extinguished whenever and however possible. Pamphlets on infant care published by the U.S. government between the 1920s and 1940s illustrate this point of view perfectly. The writers of these publications advised the mother not to pick up her baby when he cried between feedings, explaining that the baby might learn "that crying will get him what he wants, sufficient to make a spoiled fussy baby and a household tyrant whose continual demands make a slave of the mother."

Replacing this antiquated attitude with the more modern, documented concept of crying as communication is one of my objectives in this book. Time and again, I have seen this shift in parents' perspective—from seeing the cry as *irritant* to seeing it as *message*—become the first step in the quick elimination of their baby's colic. This new way of understanding the baby's cries sets the stage for a different kind of problem solving. The goal is no longer to put an end to a nerve-jangling disruption, but rather to use observation and an orderly trial-and-error program to respond appropriately to the baby's messages.

Chapter 4 will cover the actual *content* of a healthy baby's cries, and the program described in Chapter 5 will guide you in making the interpretations of and appropriate responses to the specific messages in your infant's cries. But now let's explore this new approach to crying as communication and examine how it can change the way you think about your baby's cries.

CRYING AND SPEECH DEVELOPMENT

A very brief overview of vocalization patterns over the first year or so of life can help us understand that crying is part of the gradual development of speech, the initial step on the path toward verbal communication. The newborn's cry is his or her first form of vocalization. Scientists studying the infant cry have called it "an acoustic umbilical cord," a phrase that emphasizes the function of the cry in connecting infant and parent after the physiological link between fetus and mother ends at birth. The cry serves as a signal to gain the parents' attention and concern.

The first seven weeks after birth make up *Stage 1* in the development of verbal communication, during which the cry remains the major signal. This signal is not directed at any one individual, for the infant cannot yet see other people, let alone distinguish among them. The baby simply uses his or her voice to signal into the environment when he or she is hungry, frightened, or uncomfortable. The reason for the cry is to draw an adult to the infant.

Stage 2 in the development of verbal communication is the period between eight and fourteen weeks. During this time, the infant becomes able to use the vocal cords to modify his or her vocal sounds. Now the infant has the neuromuscular control to make one- or two-syllable utterances, sounds we commonly call cooing.

Toward the end of this second stage, the baby starts directing the vocal signals to people. The baby can now see people and can perceive that it is "people" who are responding to the signals. But the baby is still not able to distinguish among individuals.

During *Stage 3*, from fifteen through thirty weeks of age, the infant can interact in simple ways with the environment. It is during this time that the baby shows a preference for the mother. Vocalizations are part of what the baby uses to interact, and these are now longer, quieter, and more variable than before. These vocal sounds are called babbling.

In *Stage 4*, from thirty-one to fifty-two weeks, the baby interacts much more vocally with the mother. Out of this increased babbling come individual words and finally speech.

In this context, it is easy to see that even the very earliest cries are primitive signals, and that though they are imprecise, their function is to link the baby with his or her parent.

THE CONTENT OF CRIES

But do the earliest cries have content? That is, do they carry specific messages? One way researchers have tried to answer this question is by determining whether cries vary in different contexts. If cries actually carry varying messages, one would expect cries to vary along with the needs they signal. By analyzing sound spectrograms of the cries of infants whose particular needs are known, researchers have indeed found that cries vary with needs. They have identified three basic cry patterns: the hunger cry, the anger cry, and the pain cry. These three cries differ from each other with respect to their melodic patterns, their length, and their frequency.

INTERPRETING THE CRYING SIGNAL

Though crying is an effective way of getting adults to respond, it is imprecise as a message and often difficult to interpret. In studies in which tapes of infant cries have been played, adults' interpretations of the cries have varied greatly. The adult's age, sex, emotional background, and previous experience with infants all appear to affect the ability to interpret the cries accurately.

In analyzing the responses of adults to infant cries, two factors seem important—the intensity and the length of the cry. The more intense and longer the cry, the more closely adults associate it with pain. The hunger, anger, and pain cries differ in intensity and length, and it is the pain cry that is the most intense and the longest. Listeners associate long, intense cries with pain, so at first glance there seems to be a perfect fit between cry and interpretation.

However, the situation is less clear-cut than it first appears. Cry analyses are done at the start of crying— that is, the tapes played are of babies just beginning an episode of crying. However, if a hungry baby is not fed, his or her crying will become more and more intense over time—*until it resembles a pain cry.* I have italicized this phrase because it is a key to our new understanding of colic. This increased intensity, which I refer to in this book as *agitation,* obscures the original meaning of the cry.

Here, then, lies the heart of the infant-adult communication problem, and not only for parents of colicky babies but for all parents. The young baby communicates through an imprecise nonverbal system that consists solely of the cry. Initially, cries of hunger, anger, and pain *might* be distinguishable with regard to their pattern, length, and intensity. But after a short time, cries of any sort become very intense and very long—identical, in fact, to a pain cry. The central difficulty becomes how to determine whether or not the crying baby is actually in pain.

RULING OUT PAIN

When you are listening to a long, intense cry, and when that cry is coming from your own baby, despite reassurances to the contrary, it is difficult to think of anything other than pain as a possible cause. And when your attempts to soothe the baby are ineffective, you will naturally think it is because your baby is in pain. In a loving parent, the infant's cries create an emotion of empathy and the urgent desire to help. The cries also raise feelings of intense concern. In considering what we can do to soothe our babies' cries, we very often begin by turning inward. That is, we identify with and project onto the baby our own understanding of what a baby's cry is for.

Adults cry when they are extremely unhappy or in pain, and usually not when they are hungry, tired, or experiencing other basic needs. In projecting their understanding of crying onto the baby, parents often imbue the infant's cries with an urgency the infant doesn't really have, imagining pain where none exists.

Given all the reasons why you might worry that your infant's cries are signaling pain, how can you be sure they are not? To begin answering this question, let me call attention to our original definition of colic: excessive crying in *healthy* infants.

Healthy infants do not have pain. A baby who does have pain does not fit our definition, for pain signals the presence of a medical problem. Yes, infants with milk allergy can have pain, but they also have vomiting and diarrhea.

The only way you can determine whether your infant is perfectly healthy and therefore free of pain is to consult your physician. This is an absolute rule and the first step in the colic prevention program described in this book.

The physician will rely on two important tools to rule out pain. The first is a careful medical history, which the doctor will get from you, and the second is a complete and thorough physical examination. So you must be as careful an observer of your infant's behavior as possible. I realize that this can be difficult when you are exhausted, anxious, and distraught, as parents often are when they have a colicky baby. Still, the physician's most important tool in making an accurate evaluation is the story you tell.

It may be helpful, therefore, to write down your daily observations. Jot down such things as any vomiting or diarrhea, constipation, cold symptoms, cough and nasal congestion, and skin rashes. Also report any medications you have given your child.

In theory, you shouldn't have to volunteer such information; the physician should ask you about these matters specifically. But very often both you and the doctor are so absorbed by the crying problem that other areas are overlooked. The story of Baby Mark will illustrate how the complexities of life with a colicky baby can make it hard for both doctor and parent to tell what's really going on.

MARK'S STORY

Mark was referred to me at four months of age because of persistent colic. His mother was a stockbroker with a very demanding job, and to make matters more complicated, she had a serious chronic gastrointestinal condition. When I saw her, she was having a relapse, which gave her a lot of pain, and she was worried about the possibility of having to go to the hospital. The stress of worrying about her baby, her job, and her own health made for a very complex emotional environment at home.

Mark's father was a builder, and he often traveled to construction sites for weeks at a time. When his mother was working, Mark stayed at the babysitter's, but during the time she was off sick, she didn't feel she could justify the expense of day care, so she kept Mark at home with her.

As for Mark's symptoms, since the age of four weeks he had had long episodes of inconsolable crying. These occurred both at the babysitter's and at home. Predictably, his pediatrician diagnosed colic and encouraged the parents to grin and bear it, promising that the crying episodes would pass when Mark was three months old.

At four months, Mark was still crying. The confusion in the household, both emotional and logistical, was overwhelming. The mother's illness, which could debilitate her with pain, was constantly upsetting the family's plans. The father's travels were unpredictable, as he was often called away to deal with unexpected emergencies. The babysitter herself added to the tension, since she wanted to be able to schedule her time and take a replacement for Mark if he wasn't going to show up consistently.

On a deeper level, the mother was uncertain about the wisdom of working full time, not only in terms of what was best for Mark but also with respect to her own health. The family's practitioner continued to reassure them that the infant's crying was normal, repeating that the syndrome was harmless and had no long-term negative effects. When Mark was two months old, the doctor had told Mark's mother it would all be over in another four weeks. At ten weeks, he told her to hang on for two more weeks and it would all seem like a bad dream. At three months, he had run out of answers. He referred Mark to the Gastroenterology Division of the Children's Hospital of Philadelphia, and that's where I met the family.

Almost immediately, the complexities of the household struck me as overwhelming: a mother with a full-time career and a debilitating gastrointestinal disease, a father with a time-consuming job that took him away for long stretches of time, an edgy babysitter, and a colicky baby. The mother not only had the usual guilt and self-questioning associated with colic, but she was worried, too, that the baby might have inherited her disease.

In a recounting of Mark's medical history, the crying seemed extreme even for infant colic—Mark was well into his fourth month and crying six to seven hours a day! I asked my usual questions, screening for medical problems. Was there any diarrhea? No. Any vomiting? No. Had Mark gained weight and grown well? Yes. Was the baby taking any medication now or had he ever in the past? Yes, Bentyl had been prescribed at two months, but it had had no effect on the crying. Did Mark have any other medical problems I should be aware of? None.

I asked that Mark be brought into the examining room for the physical exam. The baby's head, ears, nose, and throat were all normal. His chest was clear; there were no heart murmurs. To my surprise, as I felt the abdomen, I thought I detected a mass of stool on the left side, a rather unusual finding. Then I did a rectal exam and discovered that Mark was massively impacted with stool. He had the worst case of constipation I had ever seen in a four-month-old infant.

"You never mentioned that Mark had a constipation problem," I said as I continued my exam.

"Oh," she replied. "Didn't I? He did have some hard stools in the past. I mentioned it once to our doctor during a routine checkup and he suggested I give Mark Karo syrup and water."

"Did you do that?"

"Oh, yes."

I asked if the physician followed up on the problem with a phone call or a question during the next checkup. No, she replied. Had he ever performed a rectal exam?

No. Had they ever discussed Mark's constipation again? Not that she could recall.

I was sure that Mark's severe constipation accounted for his excessive crying. He certainly had abdominal cramps, but he didn't have infant colic syndrome. This was not a completely healthy baby—he had a pain-causing medical problem. I prescribed several enemas for Mark, explaining to the mother how to administer them, and then began treating the baby with a stool softener. With this medication, his stools became soft and his crying soon abated.

Mark's story serves to illustrate several points. The first is the importance of making sure your infant has no medical conditions that could cause pain before embarking on the program in this book. The program is intended only for infants with the infant colic syndrome, that is, infants who are completely healthy with excessive crying. Mark did not have the infant colic syndrome—he had a medical condition, severe constipation, which caused him pain. Second, if your infant has a medical condition that causes pain, it can be determined, as in Mark's case, with a careful history and physical examination. A normal history and physical examination eliminates this possibility. Lastly, it is important that the physician to whom you take your infant for the examination be someone who takes the symptom of excessive crying in infants *seriously*. Frequently, physicians who believe that excessive crying associated with the infant colic syndrome results from immaturity of the infant's nervous system fail to take infant crying seriously.

If Mark's story shows the pitfalls of such an attitude, another story, that of Joy McGlynn, illustrates these dangers even more dramatically.

JOY'S STORY

Mrs. McGlynn came to see me with her seven-month-old daughter, Joy, who was constantly crying. The baby had begun to have crying episodes at three weeks of age, and these gradually increased in length until, at about five weeks, they were approximately four hours long. The pediatrician Mrs. McGlynn was seeing told her there was nothing to worry about—that the baby had colic and that it would go away by about three months.

At four months, though, Joy was still crying—more than ever—and nothing Mrs. McGlynn could do would calm her. Now the pediatrician said that Joy was teething—that the cries indicated sore gums and were to be expected.

When Joy was five months old, and her crying was disrupting the household more than ever, the pediatrician called Mrs. McGlynn into his office after a well-baby check and suggested that she was being overly concerned about the crying and that perhaps she was actually "spoiling" Joy with her attentions. The doctor's intention was kindly, but there was no mistaking his message: Mrs. McGlynn was neurotic and Joy's crying was an expression of her mother's psychological problems. He reminded Mrs. McGlynn of the difficulty she had had in conceiving Joy—she had gone to a fertility specialist for three years before becoming pregnant. Now, he pointed out, her long-awaited infant simply wasn't responding to her mothering. The doctor suggested that Mrs. McGlynn was upsetting Joy with the intensity of her *need* for Joy's response to her.

Mrs. McGlynn was terribly upset by this "diagnosis" and was almost willing to accept it as an accurate assessment. Joy was crying for eight hours a day now, and Mrs. McGlynn hadn't been well rested in nearly six months. She alternated between hating the baby and hating herself for being unable to mother Joy properly. Still, she had an intuition that something was wrong with Joy—something more than merely colic or teething. At the same time, her reduced self-esteem quelled that nagging voice inside her that said things just weren't right. She felt that indeed she *was* emotionally too high-strung and that her high hopes for Joy were somehow causing the crying episodes. Mrs. McGlynn saw doctors as authority figures who were never to be questioned or doubted. So instead of discussing her uncertainties with the pediatrician, she talked to her friends about them.

Fortunately, one of Mrs. McGlynn's friends was a nurse in my office. My nurse described the situation and asked me what I thought, and I answered that Joy simply shouldn't be crying as much as she was. Something had to be done, I told her, and I would be happy to see the family in a consultation. It took a good deal of persuading for Mrs. McGlynn to see me. She felt she would be showing disloyalty to her doctor in getting a second opinion and was worried about offending him.

When Mrs. McGlynn finally brought Joy in, I examined the baby and was immediately struck by the very long, narrow shape of her head. I asked Mrs. McGlynn if the original pediatrician had mentioned this to her. She answered that he had told her that the natural openings (sutures) between the skull bones of infants seemed to be closing earlier than usual in Joy, but he hadn't seemed too concerned. In fact, he had noted that Mrs. McGlynn herself had a long, narrow head, and mentioned that this head shape was probably a familial trait.

But I suspected that Joy had a condition called craniosynostosis, in which the sutures of the skull in the developing infant fuse earlier than normal. The baby's skull is made up of five bony plates that remain unfused to allow the brain to grow, and ordinarily they begin to fuse sometime after the first year of life. In the case of craniosynostosis, the fusion takes place much earlier, usually along one seam, or suture, only. Such early joining of two of the skull's bones results in an abnormally shaped cranium, which is a cosmetic problem. Surgery to reopen the suture is used to correct the situation.

In giving me Joy's medical history, Mrs. McGlynn described Joy's constant crying, and she also told me of episodes of head banging.

What was I to make of these factors—suspected craniosynostosis, head-banging, and excessive crying? I had never associated craniosynostosis with pain, having been taught that the condition was purely a cosmetic problem. But I had before me an infant with severe excessive crying and a physical abnormality. I had to consider the possibility that they were linked. Perhaps, I thought, the closing of the sutures was causing an increase of pressure within the brain. If so, it would undoubtedly cause extreme pain.

I called the head of the Department of Neurosurgery at the Children's Hospital of Philadelphia and asked him if he knew of any link between craniosynostosis and increased pressure within the cranium. He told me some reports from France had recently described just such a connection. I told him about Joy and asked him if he thought craniosynostosis could be giving her severe headaches. He answered yes, definitely, and asked if he could see the baby. I told him I would certainly ask Mrs. McGlynn, and when I described our conversation to her, she agreed to see the neurosurgeon in consultation.

After evaluating Joy, the neurosurgeon confirmed the diagnosis of craniosynostosis. He said that her sutures had probably been closed at birth and felt sure that increased intracranial pressure was giving her pain. The corrective surgery was performed, and within two weeks Joy's crying was in the normal range for her age.

I asked Mrs. McGlynn to keep a behavior diary on Joy between the time of our first visit and her appointment with the neurosurgeon. This is a task I prescribe routinely to every family with a baby who is crying excessively (and a fundamental component in the program in this book). The diary revealed that Joy was crying on an average of seven hours a day—an astronomical amount of crying for a seven-month-old baby. Mrs. McGlynn's life must have been truly horrific over the last several months—and yet her pediatrician had suggested that she was making too much of Joy's crying.

This was indeed an extreme case of a physician failing to take infant crying seriously, and it is a clear illustration of the risk such a position entails.

My aim in telling Joy's story is neither to frighten you nor to suggest that you consider craniosynostosis as the cause of your child's colic. The condition is uncommon, and the presence of pain with it is even more so.

Instead, I am using Joy's case to urge you to take your infant to a doctor to insure he or she has no medical condition that is causing pain. Again, I urge you to take your infant to a physician who takes the symptom of excessive crying seriously and will therefore conscientiously listen to your story, as well as examine your baby.

Joy did not have the infant colic syndrome. She was not a normal, healthy baby. She had a medical condition, obvious on exam, causing her pain. Proper treatment for Joy was delayed because her physician did not consider her excessive crying as an important symptom whose cause needed to be explained.

When I evaluate an infant with excessive crying and find the history from the parents and physical examination to give no evidence of any abnormal medical condition, I am certain the infant is not crying from pain. On the other hand, physicians who automatically assume all infants with excessive crying are having abdominal pain regardless of their history and physical exam can also delay proper treatment just as much as Joy's doctor did. The following case history illustrates this point.

ALLEN'S STORY

So far I've focused on the problem of ruling out pain in learning to interpret infants' cries. Before we leave the difficulties of this and go on to discuss solutions, I want to illustrate one more risk in adhering to convention when it comes to infant colic syndrome and to show how this risk interferes with the accurate interpretation of infants' cries. In the stories of Mark and Joy, both physicians subscribed to the immature-nervous-system theory, which led them to consider pain unlikely as a cause of the babies' crying. But in the story of Allen, the doctor was a believer in the second common theory of colic—namely, that abdominal pain is present and is causing the baby's crying.

Allen Johnson was five months old when I first saw him in my office. I knew when I met his parents that his problem must be a troubling one, because they had had to drive 120 miles to see me. They told me that at three weeks of age, Allen had begun to cry excessively and inconsolably. His pediatrician diagnosed him as having colic, which he believed was caused by a milk protein allergy. I asked if any vomiting, diarrhea, constipation, or abnormality turned up in an examination, and Mrs. Johnson told me it did not. Despite Allen's lack of symptoms, the doctor held to his belief that Allen was in pain and recommended a formula change on the assumption that his formula, Similac (a cow's milk protein), was causing the crying.

The first change was to Isomil, a soy-based formula. When Mrs. Johnson reported no abatement of the crying after two weeks, the doctor ordered Nutramigen (as explained earlier, it is impossible to be allergic to this formula). Still, Allen continued to cry between four and five hours a day. So the physician tried a second soy formula, Nursoy. When that didn't work he prescribed Progestimil, similar to Nutramigen.

No change. Allen continued to cry, and the physician continued to believe that pain was causing the crying. He decided to stop blaming the formula and look to other possibilities—ulcers or heartburn. Though he did not test for the presence of these conditions, he prescribed medications for them. Two of these were antacids—Maalox and Mylanta. A third was Reglan, used to prevent stomach acid from backing up into the esophagus, where it can cause burning (heartburn).

As I was taking the history, I was privately trying to figure out what this doctor had in mind. He seemed to be hoping that if he tried enough possible solutions he'd hit on the right one. Fortunately for Allen, the Johnsons were very persistent in seeking treatment for Allen's crying. When the symptom didn't disappear, they wouldn't let the pediatrician off the hook but kept returning to him for advice. His course of action was completely dominated by his belief that colic is caused by abdominal pain. So without any evidence of such pain, he tried in turn every treatment ever described for abdominal pain in the colicky baby.

When Allen was three months old, he was still crying four to five hours a day. The textbooks say that colic goes away at three months, so when Allen still showed signs of it, his pediatrician referred him to a pediatric gastroenterologist at a major medical center in his city. The gastroenterologist, too, assumed that Allen was suffering abdominal pain and put him on an antispasmodic, Levsin. He also prescribed Phenobarbital, a medication used mostly as an anticonvulsant to prevent seizures and occasionally as a sedative. Why he chose to use it on Allen I can only guess. Perhaps he really wasn't sure what was going on and thought that putting the baby to sleep would help. Whatever his thinking, it didn't work. Every time Allen had a long bout of crying, the Johnsons called the specialist and he increased the Phenobarbital. And still it didn't work.

The Johnsons were nervous about giving Allen these medications but they didn't want to stop them, in case he had a serious gastroenterological problem. So they decided to get a second opinion. They called the Department of Gastroenterology at the Children's Hospital of Philadelphia, where they were referred to me.

Mrs. Johnson had other concerns about Allen's behavior besides the persistent crying. "He just never seems happy," she told me. "He never smiles, never coos, never laughs. He never even fusses. He just cries and cries." Mrs. Johnson, a teacher, already had a five-year-old child, so she was familiar with a normal five-month-old's behavior.

Allen's history except for the excessive crying was entirely normal, as was his physical examination. Therefore, I knew he was not crying because of abdominal pain, or pain from any other cause. I treated him with the approach described in this book, and within two weeks, his excessive crying had abated. More excitingly, Mrs. Johnson called two months later to tell me that Allen was a happy, normal seven-month-old. She told me he was smiling, laughing, cooing, babbling, fussing, and, yes, sometimes crying.

In the stories of Mark and Joy, we saw what can happen when one considers an infant's cries meaningless and unrelated to communication. Here, in Allen's story, the error is in the opposite direction. So focused were the practitioners on the idea that intense crying signifies pain that it never occurred to them that Allen's vocalization could be signaling his needs.

Allen's physician's belief that his excessive crying was from abdominal pain despite a normal history and physical exam was as nonsensical as the belief of the physicians who were caring for Mark and Joy that their crying had nothing to do with pain despite an abnormal history and physical exam.

The message is simple. Take your infant to a physician. Have him or her take a careful history and physical examination. Remember, excessive crying by itself does not mean pain. Just because the infant *appears* to be in pain, it doesn't mean the crying is from pain. If the physician takes your concern over inconsolable crying seriously and finds no medical condition in your infant that could cause pain, you can relax with the knowledge your infant is not crying because he or she is in pain.

ASSESSING YOUR DOCTOR

So far I've put you in a kind of Catch-22. I've told you that before you begin interpreting the messages in your baby's cries, you must be absolutely sure the infant is healthy, because only then can you be sure your baby is not in pain. I've also said that the only way to be sure your baby is perfectly healthy is to have a careful history and physical examination done by a pediatrician or family doctor. But then, in the three case histories I've just given, I've shown that, too often, even competent physicians are inhibited from taking accurate histories and performing accurate physical exams by the misconceptions about colic. So what are you supposed to do?

Fortunately, there is a simple way out of this dilemma: Through direct questioning, *make sure that the physician you see takes infant crying seriously.*

If you are reading this book on the suggestion of the doctor caring for your baby, the problem has already been solved. In such a case, you can be assured that your doctor takes infant crying seriously and will, in the course of taking the history and performing the exam, consider the significance of the baby's cries.

If your doctor has not mentioned this book, I suggest you make a point of having a talk to discover how he or she feels about crying and its importance. Having read this book, it will be easy for you to determine whether or not the doctor takes infant crying seriously and to identify the belief on which his or her treatment is based. Most likely, any pediatrician who does not use the concepts in this book subscribes to one of the two beliefs identified earlier: that colic is the result of an immature nervous system or that colic is the result of abdominal pain. In either case, this doctor is sure to tell you that colic is harmless and always goes away. At that point, you should mention this book's approach and discuss it with the doctor.[1]

---

1. *He or she should be familiar with the concepts discussed here, because the results of the studies I made of my treatment*

The physician's reaction to the concepts presented in this book will signal how receptive he or she will be to the idea of crying as communication and how willing he or she will be to work with you. After your talk, you will either feel confident that the physician will take a thorough history and examination or you will have misgivings. Should you be left with a lack of confidence, you should try another physician. Although you might not find a physician whose approach to colic is exactly like mine, you should be able to find one who is concerned and open-minded and who wants to work with you to help your baby.

OVERCOMING DOUBT

At this point, let's assume that you have observed your infant carefully and taken notes for the physician. You have found a doctor you have confidence in who has done a careful history and physical exam. The doctor reports that everything is normal. Are you certain, without any nagging doubt at all, that your baby is absolutely free of pain? In my experience, it is very difficult for parents to give up believing that their excessively crying babies might be in pain. As I hinted earlier, it is *instinctive* for parents to respond with alarm when a baby cries—and alarm means admitting into consciousness the possibility that the baby is in danger or pain. Since

---

approach to colic have been published in Pediatrics, *one of the journals pediatricians depend on to keep abreast of new developments in their field. Doctors who have read the reports of these studies will understand that my treatment approach has been proven effective. Knowing that the principles in this book have been tested and reported in* Pediatrics, *these doctors will consider them neither bizarre nor strange, even though they conflict with the more conventional approaches to colic they learned in medical school.*

the biggest stumbling block to effective treatment of infant colic syndrome is convincing parents that their healthy infant is crying in order to communicate rather than in reaction to pain, let me make one last point before we move on to the subject of interpreting a healthy baby's cries.

What you need as a parent is the confidence that a doctor's thorough history and careful physical examination are reliable in turning up any source of existing pain. You probably aren't aware that you already have achieved such confidence with respect to other conditions. Ear infections, for example, are among the most common medical problems pediatricians see and are certainly among the most common causes of pain in children. Once a child begins talking, the diagnosis of an ear infection is easy; the child complains of ear pain, and the doctor examines the ear to determine visually whether infection is present.

But before the child learns to talk, the process is more difficult, especially for first-time parents. In fact, with the first child, the diagnosis of an ear infection often surprises parents. Take the case of a nine-month-old who has a fever and cold symptoms and has been up all night crying. It is obvious to the parents that the child is ill, and they bring the baby in to the doctor for treatment. The crying, they assume, relates to the baby's general discomfort, and they are often surprised to learn that the baby has an ear infection and was probably crying from pain.

With a few doses of an antibiotic, the infection recedes. The baby stops crying—though the cold symptoms remain—and the parents start to take the doctor's word for it that the baby was in fact crying from ear pain. The next time the baby starts to cry, they consider ear pain a possible cause but still need to consult the doctor to know for sure. The physician examines the infant and finds no ear infection. The parents then accept the fact that this time they were only guessing when they considered ear pain a possible cause of the crying.

With infant colic syndrome, when parents become concerned that their baby is having abdominal pain, they are guessing in the same way. They base their guess on the way the infant is crying. The agitation, the hardened abdomen, the angry face, and the intensity of the voice all suggest pain to them. But, as a pediatrician, once I do a history and examination and find no abnormalities and no symptoms other than the crying itself, I can conclude with as much confidence as when I see a clear, healthy eardrum that the crying baby is not in pain.

INTERPRETING THE MESSAGE

If, as I have stated, colicky infants are not in pain but are crying to communicate their needs, why are they inconsolable? Why do they cry on and on for hours?

Let's go back to our original explanation of colic:

1. The baby cries, sending a specific message to the care-giver regarding a basic need.

2. The care-giver misinterprets the message and fails to meet the need signaled by the cry.

3. The baby's frustration leads to agitation so great that he or she is now unable to respond when the care-giver makes the accurate response.

The answer to our questions lies in Step 3. It's a simple concept, but one that many parents respond to, understandably, with frustration and even anger. "What could my baby want if she isn't in pain? Don't you think I've tried everything? I've tried feeding, walking, burping, changing, rocking, and giving a pacifier. I've even dragged the stroller into the house and pushed it around for hours at night. There's simply no need I haven't thought of, no 'answer to a message' I haven't given. Do you think I'm stupid? Of *course* I've attended to the baby's needs. This child *must* be in pain. There's no other possible explanation."

Initially an infant cries as an attempt to communicate a particular need. When the parent does not respond, either by letting the baby cry or by responding with an action that doesn't address the specific need signaled, the crying continues.

At this point, some infants would simply give up and become quiet. Infants with infant colic syndrome, however, are very determined individuals. Their temperament is such that they don't give up easily when their signals go unmet. They will cry until they are "blue in the face." And the longer they cry, the more the message will be mixed with frustration and desperation. Sooner or later, these babies become so agitated that they are unable to stop crying or even acknowledge the parents' then-accurate response to the original message. Like a three-year-old child who has awakened from a nightmare and needs five or ten minutes of soothing before feeling safe once more, the colicky baby is all agitation. And, like the forgotten nightmare, the infant's message has become lost in the commotion of feeling. Let's look at a hypothetical example to see how this happens.

BILLY'S STORY

Lois Atkinson feeds her infant, Billy, and then burps him, bathes him, dresses him, and puts him down to sleep with no problem. Billy sleeps quietly for one hour and then begins to cry—because he is hungry. Lois and her husband, Tom, not sure why Billy is crying, look at the clock and decide the baby needs more sleep. They decide to let him cry for a bit in the hope that he will drift off once more. The hungry baby cries as loudly as he can for ten minutes. Then Tom goes into Billy's room, turns on the light, and sees the infant drawing up his legs, turning red, hardening his abdomen, and passing gas. He concludes that Billy must be having gas pains and walks the baby for ten minutes.

Still hungry, Billy continues to cry. He has now been crying continuously for twenty minutes. Lois and Tom still don't consider the possibility that Billy might be hungry, because he only finished feeding an hour and twenty minutes ago. So they try a pacifier, but the baby, hungrier than ever, spits it out after sucking on it for thirty seconds and resumes crying. Now the parents put him in the swing for ten minutes, again to no avail.

Billy has now been crying for *thirty* minutes and is frustrated, angry, and extremely agitated. Exasperated, Lois puts Billy to her breast, but after trying without success for several minutes to urge the red-faced, screaming baby to suck, she gives up, feeling confident she was right in her original belief—that the baby wasn't hungry. Much as she wants not to believe it, she starts to suspect that Tom was right, that Billy is in pain for some reason.

Tom and Lois take turns walking the baby and putting him back in the crib, and after crying *for another hour,* the exhausted Billy finally falls asleep. Tom and Lois ardently hope that whatever mysterious pain has caused this tremendous outpouring of distress has disappeared by itself, and exhausted and still worried, they fall into bed themselves.

These parents would certainly describe their baby during this episode as inconsolable. They would be accurate in reporting that they tried to respond to every possible need. They tried feeding, walking, and offering the pacifier; they tried placing Billy in the swing and talking to him—all to no effect. In the conventional view, both parents and physician would describe Billy's condition as excessive inconsolable crying.

But look closely. In this scenario, Billy was forced by his parents to be inconsolable because they did not respond to his cries with feeding until he was crying for half an hour. By then, he was too agitated to calm down and feed. Had Lois and Tom assumed that the cry was one of communication and quickly addressed the possible needs in turn, they would have met the specific need Billy was signaling before he became agitated, thus avoiding the entire episode.

WHY COLIC GOES AWAY BY ITSELF

Does colic really go away by three months of age? And if so, why?

As I have mentioned, I have seen babies well beyond the three-month limit who have had infant colic syndrome. However, it is true that the majority of cases of excessive crying do decrease with time, and some completely disappear on their own by three months of age, or at least the crying reduces to a tolerable level by this time. However, in a small number of cases, the crying continues unabated.

What accounts for the diminishing if not, as the standard argument goes, the maturing of the baby's nervous system? Three factors contribute to the spontaneous decrease in crying. One is that over time, parents unconsciously try different responses to their crying infants, finally hitting on the right response. In my studies of infant colic syndrome, I have found this to occur even when the parents assume the crying is caused by pain or nonspecific irritability. I've seen them solve their problem by feeding the baby more frequently, picking the baby up sooner, or putting the baby in a swing.

MATTHEW'S STORY

The Jacob family, who participated in one of my colic studies, is a good example. Mrs. Jacob breast-fed Matthew, who cried inconsolably for long periods during the day. She suspected that Matthew was having abdominal pain. She handled him according to her pediatrician's recommendations, which were to feed the baby on demand, though never more frequently than every three hours. On entering the study, Matthew was crying between two and two and a half hours a day.

As part of my study, I put Mrs. Jacob on a milk-free diet to determine whether there was any relationship between her diet and the baby's symptoms. I also had the Jacobs keep a diary of the baby's behavior over the next nine days and asked them to continue with their handling of Matthew unchanged.

The diary showed that during the first six days of the study, Matthew began crying two to two and a half hours after a feeding. Following the original physician's directions, Mrs. Jacob would try to avoid feeding the baby by walking with him until three hours had passed since the previous feeding. But by this time, the baby would have been crying for half an hour or more and would be too agitated to feed. The resulting crying would last an hour to an hour and a half. However, after the sixth day, without any instruction from me, Mrs. Jacob started ignoring the physician's advice and began feeding Matthew before the three hours were up. When the infant would begin crying two to two and a half hours after the feeding, she would simply put him to the breast. The baby would feed readily and no crying would result. The change in the household was dramatic.

A second reason colic improves over time is that parents stop following the poor advice they have been receiving. In some cases, parents simply don't take the doctor's advice in the first place. This is especially true when the doctor advises the parents to ignore the infant's cries. Parents generally find it difficult, if not impossible, to listen to their baby's cries for hours without responding in some way, and they often rely on intuition to defy strict guidelines from the doctor.

Finally, babies change. Many things happen to the infant developmentally in the first three months of life to make him or her less demanding over time. During this period, for instance, the baby's sleeping time at night increases. By the age of three months, the majority of infants sleep uninterruptedly from at least eleven at night to four in the morning and often longer. Thus, even if the amount of daytime crying does not decrease, parents are able to tolerate it better as time goes on, because they are getting more sleep at night.

Similarly, the number of feedings the child needs during the day decreases after three months. And infants become more aware of their environment and can therefore spend more time alone without stimulation. So while parents are learning to trust their intuitions and observations, the infant's wants and needs are changing. The result is the fine-tuning of a system of communication in which needs and responses become more closely matched.

As with every aspect of human interaction, no timetable applies equally to every case. Human variation influences infant-parent interaction as much as it shapes the relations among adults. For this reason, we cannot afford to take the old-fashioned, passive route of simply waiting colic out. Too many parents are devastated when they see no easing of the chaos of colic after their children cross the magic three-month line.

IS COLIC MY FAULT?

Let's turn now to the question of why colic occurs with some babies and not with others and to the concerns that are bound to arise—especially for parents who are exhausted and distraught. Misgivings and worries such as the following are not uncommon:

- I'm doing something wrong. I don't know enough about raising a baby.

- I never should have had a baby. I'm not cut out for this.

- I can't stand to listen to this another minute. I thought I was going to love this baby so, and now all I want to do is run away.

- Somehow I'm making this baby cry and I can't even figure out how.

- In some way or another, I'm letting my baby know that I want to go back to work. I'm bored staying home all day, and listening to this constant crying isn't helping matters at all.

- I've never heard of a baby who didn't calm down when his mother picked him up. My baby doesn't like me, or else why would he still be crying in my arms?

- I just don't love the baby enough and she can tell. I thought having her was going to be the greatest thing that ever happened to me and it's turning out to be just about the worst.

Superficially, my explanation for the infant colic syndrome would seem to support the idea that the problem is your fault. But I have never for one second considered infant colic syndrome to be the parents' fault—or anyone's fault. Assigning blame in this situation is not only counterproductive, it is a gross oversimplification of a complex interaction of factors—none of which relates to the quality of the parents' love of their baby.

Parents with two, three, or four easily comforted babies can and often do come up with an inconsolable crier on the next go-around. That in itself should lay to rest any hint of parental blame. But perhaps more to the point, as I mentioned earlier, the parents of the colicky infants I have worked with are in fact unusual in the interest and concern they show for their babies' comfort and well being. They refuse to give up on the problem even when they are being advised to wait it out, and they are doing so out of an intuitive concern for the infant-parent attachment. They care about the quality of their relationships with their babies from the very beginning and will go to great lengths to ensure that this quality is high. Many parents, exhausted from and anxious about the excessive crying of their babies, have confided to me that they fear they are "bad" parents, don't love their babies enough, or have emotional problems that are somehow interfering with their parenting. But it's been my experience they are intelligent, caring, and loving parents unwilling to accept the idea that excessive crying is "normal" or "to be expected." They enter into treatment with enthusiasm, are a pleasure to work with, and achieve good results easily. The fact that you have taken the trouble to read this book, to learn more about your infant, and to ease his or her crying places you squarely in this category of responsible, caring parents.

THREE INTERACTING FACTORS

Temperament

The fact that infant colic syndrome occurs in some families but not in others is an unfortunate combination of three factors. The first and perhaps most significant factor, but one that is often overlooked, is the baby's unique temperament. Some infants are very easygoing, even falling back to sleep after a bit of fussing when they are hungry and unfed. But others come equipped with a persistent and determined temperament. These babies will start to cry when a need begins to arise and become agitated so quickly that they are unable to respond when the parents do meet the specific need.

In this same vein, some babies' cries are easier to interpret than others. For example, some infants are so extremely regular in their eating and sleeping habits that the meaning of the signals they send their parents in the form of cries is crystal clear. "Oh, five-fifteen? Baby's hungry." Some babies sleep for most of the day and night, up to eighteen out of twenty-four hours. These infants basically just sleep and eat. Their desires are quite consistent, and interpreting their cries is relatively easy. Also, these children demand less of their parents, which means that the parents are often more rested. A well-rested, clear-headed parent has a much better chance of interpreting infant cries correctly than one suffering sleep deprivation.

But some infants are extemely irregular in their feeding and sleeping, which increases the difficulty of interpreting their cries. Lots of babies sleep only eleven or twelve hours of the twenty-four. They demand a lot more time and attention than the eighteen-hour sleepers, and they constantly signal their different needs by fussing and crying during their long waking time. Not only is the interpretation of these many cries difficult in that they occur often and irregularly, but the parents making the efforts are more fatigued, which means their ability to respond is reduced.

To put these differences in context, think of the adults you know who eat three meals a day, always at the same time, go to sleep at ten-thirty on the nose, and awaken every morning thirty seconds before seven o'clock, Monday through Sunday. Now think of the less regular types you know, people who snack all day long because they get hungry at unpredictable times, who may take a nap once in a while because they get tired, but who have such energetic weeks sometimes that they get only two or three hours of sleep at night. Whatever it is that determines the individual patterns in these contrasting ways of life, we would all agree that it has nothing to do with how much their parents loved them or how "competent" their parents were as parents. We are willing to grant that these people simply differ from one another.

It is important to remember, though in fact we often forget, that babies are unique individuals too, and that expecting them to conform to specifications on how babies should act not only diminishes the delight we take in their uniqueness, but also generates unnecessary anxiety over their differences.

Parents' Expectations versus Baby's Preferences

Parental expectations, sometimes shaped by previous child-rearing experiences, can also be involved in contributing to the creation of infant colic syndrome. Consider the Kaufmans, who liked to hold their infant until she fell asleep. These parents had two older daughters, both of whom as infants fell asleep in their parents' arms every evening at bedtime. But the new infant, Caryn, cried at bedtime and could not be consoled no matter what her parents did. Finally, after two months of walking Caryn to no avail, in exasperation, Mrs. Kaufman put her down in her crib one night and let her cry. Within three minutes, Caryn was asleep. In this way, she was expressing her preference for going to bed in her crib, not her mother's arms. The Kaufmans were assuming that Caryn preferred what their older daughters had responded to, and this assumption inhibited their impulse to experiment with Caryn to discover the baby's own preference.

Caryn was not only unique, she was also very determined. Built into her temperament was a persistent streak. Holding a tired baby with such a temperament when she wants to be put down will result in a great deal of crying. A natural reaction to such crying is to hold the baby close and to walk with her, only making the baby cry more.

Whenever the parents' assumptions regarding an aspect of the baby's life—eating, sleeping, or activity while awake—are at cross purposes with the baby's own preference, there is a potential for infant colic syndrome to develop. A hearty respect for the possibilities that the infant has his or her own desires could lead to a solution that nips the problem of inconsolable crying in the bud.

Well-Meant Advice

The third factor that can inhibit the accurate interpretation of a baby's cries and therefore lead to infant
colic syndrome was touched upon in Chapter 2—the advice to new parents that friends and family give so freely.
Parents who are new at the game and understandably
unsure of themselves often accept well-intended advice
as gospel. They see it as coming from the very well of
experience without considering the possibility that it
might be mixed with myth and inaccuracies. But, as I
suggested earlier, because colic has been around for so
long and because its effects on the household can be so
devastating, much of the advice parents receive from
concerned loved ones is just that—rooted in myth and
fashion rather than scientific proof.

I covered the common myths surrounding colic earlier. Here let me briefly note the consequences of accepting without question the three common categories of free
advice you'll find circulating. The first, which I covered
extensively earlier, is that all excessive crying is associated with abdominal pain. If you accept this myth, you
will stop trying to interpret the meaning of your baby's
cries and will go on a wild goose chase searching for the
cause of the "pain" you assume is there. You will change
formulas, change your diet if you are breast-feeding,
change feeding and sleeping schedules, ask your doctor
for medication—all to no avail. Your baby will still be
sending you specific signals of his or her particular need
while you look for a way to end the "pain."

The second prevalent myth, which I also thoroughly
discussed earlier, is that all babies have fussy periods,
some longer than others. "There's nothing you can do
about it," the wisdom goes, "so don't even try. Besides,
it's harmless and they always outgrow it." The underlying message here is "just let the baby cry." Again, if you
accept it, you will stop trying to understand your baby's

messages to you on the assumption that nonspecific irritability, not a particular need, is causing the crying.

The third myth says that if you respond every time
your baby cries, you will "spoil" the child; that the infant's
crying is meant to manipulate you into giving the child
too much attention. People who offer this advice urge
you to be firm, hold your ground, and wait for the crying
to pass.

Very young infants demand great attention, but not
because they're plotting to steal it. They demand attention because they *require* it. Our biological system of pro-
creation is designed that way. Unlike babies of some other
species, our infants are fully dependent on adults until
their complex physiological, intellectual, motor, psychological, and emotional development has reached the
point—years down the line—when our offspring can function autonomously. Without constant attention, our infants would not survive. Their cries are the means by
which they ensure that they get that needed attention.

THE COMBINATION

These three factors—infant temperament, parental
expectations, and poor advice—can combine in a way
that results in infant colic syndrome. Unless you learn
the principles and apply the program described in this
book, whether or not your infant develops colic will be
more a result of chance than of your particular parenting
style. My own family is a perfect example.

Our first baby, a daughter named Yael, was born while
I was a pediatric resident at the Children's Hospital of
Philadelphia, and there I was taught the prevailing—but
incorrect—immature-nervous-system theory of colic.

Of course, I explained this approach in detail to my
wife as if it were the received law. And there were times
late at night when Yael seemed awake and alert after a

feeding, times when I believed she should be sleeping. It was, after all, two in the morning, and both my wife and I needed our sleep. During these episodes, I would insist that we put the baby to sleep, and I vividly remember my wife and myself cringing in our bed while the baby cried behind her closed bedroom door.

Fortunately for us, this little girl had an easygoing, flexible temperament. After ten minutes of crying, she would slip off to sleep and my wife and I would finally be able to relax. But those ten-minute episodes were really excruciating for us. If your baby has been crying straight from six to ten o'clock every evening for the last three months, or on and off for hours throughout the day and night, you might laugh at our sensitivity and call us greenhorns. But we found even those brief crying spells difficult and full of anxiety.

I was so well trained in the immature-nervous-system theory that I can well imagine what would have happened had our child had a different temperament and had she cried inconsolably without giving up. As the crying passes the ten-minute mark, I can picture my wife and myself beginning to argue about picking her up. My wife says yes. Citing the pediatric experts, I say emphatically no. I see my wife, very much against her better judgment, finally giving in to the wisdom of the medical establishment, whose experience in such matters she trusts more than she does her first-time mother's intuition.

Finally, after half an hour of talking it out while the baby works herself into a new level of intensity, now screaming and passing gas, I see my wife throwing caution to the wind, saying she doesn't care a bean what my colleagues would say, and hurrying to pick up Yael. But by now the baby is so agitated that nothing will quiet her and she is firmly embarked on a course of crying that alternately scares us, exasperates us, sends us into a new round of arguments, and keeps us awake until three in the morning. Later in the morning, exhausted, I tell my fellow pediatric residents that my baby has come down with colic.

By the time our second baby, Naomi, came along, I had learned that an infant's cries are far more than just a wall of sound to be ignored. Judging from the single-mindedness of our second daughter in achieving her personal goals in her childhood years, I'd say we were lucky my experience with my first child had taught me to listen and think about infant communication rather than to close the door on it. Otherwise, we would have been in for some very long nights. This was a girl who *would be heard*. Since some elements of people's personalities seem to be discernible from the very first days after birth, I have no doubt that this daughter would have found a way to get her message across no matter how long it took. Letting her cry surely would have resulted in colic.

So you see, the reason my first daughter was not colicky was not brilliant parenting but simple luck. We had two of the three factors necessary for colic—incorrect assumptions and poor advice—but fortunately the third, the determined and tenacious temperament, was not there. By the time our second daughter came along, we had changed the first two factors in order to cope with the third—we had the determined, tenacious baby but were free of misconceptions so we could respond directly to the messages in her cries.

SUMMARY

Reiterating the basic principles elaborated in this chapter will ensure that you understand what is happening when your colicky baby cries.

- Infant colic syndrome is a condition in which healthy infants *usually* under three months of age have excessive, inconsolable crying (*seemingly* inconsolable would actually be more accurate) of an unknown cause.

- The infant cries at first to communicate his or her specific wants and needs.

- Initially, the parents misinterpret the specific cause of the crying and inadvertently offer the wrong response.

- The infants' temperament is such that he or she continues to cry, soon becoming too agitated to stop crying even when the parents offer the correct response to the original message.

The solution is for parents to learn to interpret their infants' cries as accurately as possible. The next chapter will describe in detail the messages in your healthy baby's cries.

Chapter 4
Why Healthy Babies Cry

Healthy babies cry for one or a combination of five reasons only—to signal:

- The need for food

- The need for sleep

- The need to suck

- The need to be held

- The need for stimulation

In this chapter, I will cover these fundamental needs in detail. I'll present the most recent scientific data bearing on these needs and dispel the myths and misconceptions surrounding them. This information will make it easy to apply the colic-prevention program described in Chapter 5. As a result, I can assure you that you and your baby will spend many of the hours now spent in anxiety, concern, and mutual frustration enjoying each other's company in a more peaceful atmosphere.

THE NEED FOR FOOD

Babies cry when they are hungry; this is certainly something everybody knows. But many possible concerns and misconceptions can interfere with the parents' realization that their baby is hungry; these same concerns and misconceptions can make parents reluctant to feed the infant even when they do realize the child is hungry.

How Much Is Just Right?

One source of misconception is how much to feed the baby. Many would answer with what seems obvious: Give the baby as much as she needs to satisfy her. But this is not always as simple as it sounds.

For example, Joe and Marcia had their first baby, David, in their mid-thirties. Marcia had had a weight problem all her life, and now, after her first pregnancy, was distressed to discover that controlling her weight was even more difficult than it used to be. Her father had often ridiculed her for being overweight and frequently said, "What? Eating? Again?" But at the same time, he had also taught her to eat rich foods, reward herself with heavy meals and ice cream, and comfort herself during difficult times with high-caloric treats. Joe, on the other hand, slim by nature, considered Marcia's weight to be perfect, and had no patience with her self-criticism whenever she felt she had gained too much weight.

Then along came David, one ounce short of ten pounds at birth and 21 inches! "What a beefy baby!" Marcia overheard someone say at the store, and she was crushed. Her doctor unknowingly reinforced her anxiety by suggesting that David was "off the charts" in terms of weight gain in the first month after birth.

Marcia kept up with current events, and what she read in the newspaper didn't help to allay her anxiety over David's steady weight gain. Feature articles in the health section reported new findings that "fat babies mean fat adults." Marcia felt a desperate need to slow down David's weight gain, for which she somehow felt responsible. She bemoaned David's fate in having obviously inherited her tendency to put on weight.

The physician was also concerned about David's weight and, after monitoring David's weight gain for two months, decided to prescribe a controlled feeding regimen. "Feed him no more than every three hours. You can give him water in between, but no milk, and no more than thirty-two ounces of formula a day."

So Marcia began a scheduled feeding approach and grimly took the consequences: David's outrage, loudly expressed for long, long periods of time.

There was no mystery about why David was crying. He was *hungry* and his parents knew it. Finally, after several weeks, she gave in to her intuition, which told her she was responding more to her own internal discomfort about body weight than to her baby's specific needs. She went to a highly recommended pediatrician in her area for a second opinion, and after a long consultation was able to admit to her anxiety that David might be obese all his life. The doctor assured her that David's weight gain was perfectly normal for a baby of David's length.

The doctor advised Marcia to return to David's previous schedule and predicted that his weight gain would soon level off. This indeed proved to be the case. Even before the leveling off took place, Marcia and Joe concluded that they had done the right thing. David's temperament returned to its original placid evenness and the atmosphere in the household went from the anxious concern that excessive crying creates to the warmth that surrounds a secure baby in the pink of health.

The newspaper articles that Marcia read came to be written because of two theories that were popular in the late 1970s. One study showed a strong correlation between obesity at six months of age and obesity later on in life. The other suggested that obese people of any age had more fat cells than nonobese people and that the number of fat cells becomes fixed in early life. Thus, these investigators reported, someone who is obese in infancy is destined to have a higher than normal number of fat cells throughout life and will therefore *most likely* remain fat permanently.

Further research has disputed both of these theories. But the disproving of a theory, especially one about fat, is not nearly as appealing to the popular media as reports of a new theory explaining why fat Americans are fat. So the disproving of these theories received only a fraction of the attention the original dramatic propositions enjoyed. Nevertheless, recent well-designed studies have shown that there is no correlation between size—both in height and weight—at six months of age and later on in life. To be sure, there *is* a correlation between childhood and adult obesity, but not until after infancy.

Most nutritionists agree that infants do a good job of regulating their own caloric intake if allowed to do so—a fact that supports *demand feeding* (feeding the infant as much formula or breast milk as wanted, whenever it's wanted), a technique that has been as vulnerable in the last few generations to the whims of fashion as skirt length. Today, experts agree that demand feeding is the only way to proceed in early infancy, and the program presented in this book incorporates this belief.

What do we mean by saying that babies can control their caloric intake? Simple. Both breast- and bottle-fed babies will feed when they are hungry and stop feeding when they are full. Some physicians, like David's, mistakenly think they need to put a limit on the amount of formula a baby is fed. As in David's case, they usually tell parents not to feed over thirty-two ounces of formula per day. This practice makes no sense at all. The average amount of formula a three-month-old infant drinks is thirty-two ounces. But, a baby who is above average in length will most likely need an above average amount of formula per day. An infant's daily caloric needs are dependent on his or her size, activity level, and resting metabolic rate. No physician can know these factors for a particular baby. Fortunately, the infant knows how much he or she needs. There are two ways to make use of this self-controlling mechanism to avoid overfeeding your baby.

First, do not feed your baby solid food before six months of age. The reason for this is simple but rarely recognized. Young infants do not have enough head or neck control to show that they want more food or to refuse solid food when they are full. That is, they cannot lean forward and open their mouths to feed when they are hungry and cannot close their mouths and turn their heads away when they are full. So the self-controlling mechanism cannot function when the infant is being fed solid foods. And since the formula or breast milk meets all the child's nutritional needs until the six-month mark, feeding the child solid food before that time is really a cultural habit, not a nutritional necessity.

The second means of avoiding overfeeding might seem too obvious to mention, but given the prevalence and power of preconceptions in matters of child rearing, it makes good sense to state it explicitly. *Avoid overfeeding—that is, do not force the bottle or breast on the baby.* If an infant stops sucking and begins to fuss, he or she is communicating the message that the meal is over.

If you are not giving your infant baby food or forcing milk on the baby, you are doing everything a parent can do to prevent obesity in the first six months of life. And if, while you control his or her intake in this way, your baby is chubby at four months of age, this does not mean you will have a fat child or that the child will become a fat adult. Don't let your imagination present you with worries that are completely unsubstantiated by scientific study. Take pleasure in the robustness of your baby and enjoy it for what it is: a sign of the child's well being.

Many parents have told me that their doctors have advised them to limit their baby's milk intake to thirty-two ounces a day. Setting such an arbitrary limit on a baby's milk intake is illogical and is guaranteed to lead to unnecessary crying in babies whose bodies require more. A baby who is in the ninetieth percentile for length (that is, a baby who is longer than 90 percent of all babies of the same age) will need more calories and therefore more milk than a baby who is in the tenth percentile (shorter than 90 percent of all babies of the same age). Thirty-two ounces of milk a day may be appropriate for an average-sized baby, but it may not be nearly enough for an extremely large child. It is unfair to limit the intake of a hungry baby arbitrarily, and doing so could even have a harmful effect on the baby's growth.

Parents worry, too, about babies who are moderate feeders, and often are concerned that the child is just not eating enough. The proof is in the growth charts: A child who is healthy and gaining steadily is eating enough even if the intake at each feeding is small and doesn't conform to some set external standard, such as the thirty-two ounces. Here again, we see the power of preconception to create anxiety even when solid evidence exists to the contrary. A couple who believes that only a chubby baby is a thriving baby often needs some serious convincing in order to give up their worry.

Another stubborn misconception is that feeding a baby will always stop the baby's cries. Absolutely untrue. If a bottle is offered to a crying baby who is not hungry, the infant might stop crying momentarily, but will soon begin again. By all means, always feel comfortable about offering milk to your crying baby with the thought that the cause for the crying might be hunger. But keep in mind the possibility that there are four other needs that could be motivating the crying. If the baby is crying to be fed, he or she will greedily take the milk and become happy. But if there is another reason for the crying, expect the baby to calm down momentarily only to begin crying again.

When to Feed the Baby

Here we come face to face with the controversy of "demand" versus "scheduled" feeding. The experts support the view that there is absolutely no benefit to feeding at regular intervals rather than when the baby calls for food. Babies on an externally imposed schedule do not have less gas or fewer intestinal problems than infants fed on demand—a myth commonly cited to support scheduled feeding. Nor do they have fewer episodes of diarrhea or vomiting—another myth. Nor do such babies grow better than demand-fed babies. There is no correlation between demand feeding and obesity, or between demand feeding and future infant temperament—two more stubborn myths with no basis in fact.

So why do people continue to believe in the scheduled feeding technique? The following three myths still exist, and I believe cause the most grief in families trying to feel their way through those first few months with their new babies.

•**Myth 1:** *When babies are on a feeding schedule, life is much easier for the parents.*

•**Myth 2:** *Any baby can be put on a regular schedule of feeding with relative ease.*

•**Myth 3:** *Babies on scheduled feedings are happier and healthier than babies fed on demand.*

I've tried to stress in this book so far that parents of newborns are extremely vulnerable. "Feeling their way," hardly describes the complexity of getting to know a new human being who has only one, and an extremely imprecise, way of communicating his needs and who is completely dependent on his parents for survival. There is no way to overstate the sense of responsibility that accompanies new parenthood—and although the intensity of this feeling is perhaps diminished with the arrival of each subsequent child, it's safe to say that parents feel it anew each time they have a baby. For this reason, parents of newborns are often easily persuaded by the arguments of those around them who have already been through the complex experience they face. Transmitting acquired information from one generation to another and from one geographical region to another is what culture is all about. Still, to avoid making the same mistakes over and over across the generations, we must all remain aware that information can be inaccurate and that beliefs must be constantly checked against new, accumulating knowledge. So I urge you to receive the well-intended information from those who care about you with gratitude plus the impulse to test its accuracy against the most up-to-date empirical knowledge.

My research has shown that it is completely untrue that all babies are easily placed on a feeding schedule. Given this fact, we can safely conclude that parents who try to do so and meet with resistance do *not* have an easier life than those whose babies are on demand feeding. In fact, we can conclude that such parents are very often living with the anxiety and other emotions that accompany infant colic syndrome.

In reality, babies vary tremendously in their responses to regular feeding schedules, and success at imposing a schedule has much more to do with the baby than the parents. Some babies behave as if they have internal clocks and feed spontaneously at extremely regular intervals, as do many adults. Other babies, if allowed, will be more irregular about when they want to feed, but will still be quite flexible and easygoing even when their particular desires go unmet for a time. If they cry to be fed at three in the afternoon but are not fed, these infants will stop crying on their own after a few minutes or in response to a little distraction. It's not at all difficult to put such babies on a feeding schedule, but the credit goes to the baby, not the parents.

It's important to make this distinction, because Myth 2 carries with it a judgment about the parents' self-discipline and tenacity that can be crushing to the parents despite the fact that it is complete nonsense. There is an implied judgment in the statements that (1) all babies are easy to feed on schedule and (2) not all parents manage to place their babies on a feeding schedule—and in that judgment another myth manages to worm its way in. This myth—call it Myth 4—is that parents who don't succeed in placing their babies on schedule *spoil* their babies by overindulging them.

Let me wipe the slate clean of these myths here and now by reiterating that any parents' success in placing any baby on a feeding schedule has more to do with the baby's *temperament and/or internal hunger regulator* than with the self-discipline and determination of the parents.

Besides the naturally regular feeder and the easygoing, easily distracted babies who would prefer irregular feeding, there is a third very large group of infants who become hungry at irregular intervals and who are temperamentally very tenacious and determined. When these infants cry when they are hungry and are not fed, they will continue to cry—and cry and cry. They will not be distracted and they will not be placated, and a parent who tries to put an infant in this category on a scheduled feeding will have to listen to a great deal of crying.

With these tenacious babies, life becomes more unpleasant, not easier, for the parents when they try to impose a feeding schedule. Sometimes the child ends up showing signs of infant colic syndrome and life can become unbearable. The difference between a lot of crying and the excessive crying that marks infant colic syndrome is the agitation that makes the baby unable to feed when the breast or bottle is finally offered.

If the baby has worked him- or herself into this state of agitation and is too upset to feed, even though hunger was the original need motivating the crying, the parents may become very confused. It is at this point that they might consider the possibility of some undetermined pain to explain the crying—and soon they are hypothesizing about gas, abdominal pain, and other such causes. In their confusion, which is made worse by the crying, they turn their attention to these possibilities and away from the real cause of the crying: the feeding schedule imposed on a first hungry, but then agitated, infant.

As hinted in Marcia and Joe's case, some physicians recommend demand feeding with certain limitations. They suggest that you feed your infant *on demand as long as you do not feed more frequently than every three hours*. This is certainly more flexible than the most common feeding schedule, which is every four hours, but there are any number of babies who will find this schedule too rigid. These babies will cry and cry if not fed two-and-a-half and even two hours after a feeding. Certain doctors hold that no baby needs to be fed more than every three hours and that feeding any more frequently is too demanding on the mother. But some infants just prefer to eat more frequently. And some infants have that tenacious temperament that keeps them crying until they get what they want. I guarantee that this combination will be harder on the mother, and the whole household, than any pattern of demand feeding, no matter how erratic it might be. To avoid such a situation, I suggest you feed your infant when he or she cries to be fed.

Breast-Feeding and Milk Supply

With respect to interpreting infant cries, breast-feeding involves special considerations. Nursing mothers frequently worry that they may not be producing enough breast milk for their babies. They wonder whether their infants' frequent demands to feed might not be related more to poor milk supply than to infant temperament. Anxiety over the adequacy of the breast milk supply can in itself interfere with milk production, creating a self-fulfilling prophecy, so such concerns need to be addressed right away.

It's not difficult to determine whether your breasts are producing milk at all. You can hand-express or use a hand pump and then examine the color of what you have expressed. Colostrum, the fluid produced by the breasts after birth in the few days before milk production begins, is clear; milk, of course, is white. Also pay attention to the change in your breasts before and after a feeding to reassure yourself with respect to your milk production. It is normal for the breasts to feel full after your infant has gone without feeding for three or four hours. After the feeding, the breasts should feel less full.

Another reassuring sign is the leaking of breast milk from one breast when the infant is nursing on the other. This is evidence that the "let-down" reflex that permits effective breast-feeding has occurred. This physiologic reflex occurs in response to the infant's sucking, which causes the hypothalamus, an area of the brain, to release the hormone oxytocin into the bloodstream. When this hormone reaches the breasts, it causes the breast glands to contract, which in turn expresses milk from the nipples.

Note, by the way, that I don't recommend using a breast pump to determine the quantity of your breast milk. Use of the pump can be misleading, for it is not unusual for women with ample breast milk to obtain only an ounce or less of milk using a pump (either electric or hand). This is probably explained by the fact that the let-down response, though present during feeding, may not occur in response to the pump.

Of course, the most direct evidence that breast-feeding is successful and that your breast milk is sufficient is the baby's weight gain. Periodic weight checks showing the baby's gain will tell you that you are producing enough milk for your baby. However, if you are worried about your milk supply, don't wait for a routine visit. See your infant's doctor to have the baby weighed and discuss at that time any breast-feeding problems you may be having.

Even when your milk supply is sufficient overall, there can be low periods during particular times of the day. If your baby cries excessively late in the day on a regular basis, try to express milk to make sure you are producing then. It may be that your milk supply is at a low at this particular time of day. It sometimes happens that the nursing mother's milk supply decreases as the day goes on so that there is not enough milk for the baby in the evening. This happens most frequently in very active women, especially if they are physically exhausted, but tension and anxiety can also contribute to dips in milk production. If you suspect that there are low points in your milk-producing cycle, offer the infant a bottle of either pumped breast milk or formula immediately *after* nursing to see whether he or she is still hungry. If the baby won't take the bottle from you, try having someone else offer the bottle. Many breast-fed babies will settle for nothing less than the breast from the mother while readily accepting the alternative from another care-giver. If, in this situation, the crying is unrelated to insufficient breast milk, the infant will refuse the bottle from both you and other care-givers and will continue to cry. But if the crying was caused by hunger owing to insufficient breast milk, the baby will take one or two ounces of milk and will stop crying. If you have this experience, talk with your doctor or a nursing counselor.

The Gastrocolic Reflex

Healthy babies, both breast- and bottle-fed, sometimes cry in the middle of feeding not because they are full but because they are having slight and passing cramps. If parents are not aware of this phenomenon and do not understand its cause, they can misinterpret their infant's cries and become very confused. I describe this normal cramping here so that you can recognize it and consider it as a possible option when your baby cries briefly. As you will see, these quick-to-leave cramps are quite distinct from the sorts of cramping imagined by those who ascribe infant colic syndrome to abdominal pain. These are mild, fleeting, and associated with eating.

Such cramping is the result of a phenomenon called the gastrocolic reflex. This is a normal response to eating that occurs in all of us from infancy through adulthood. When food enters the stomach, a hormone is released that causes the rectum to contract. In adults, there is usually some delay between eating and the beginning of rectal contractions. This is what gives us the urge to have a bowel movement shortly after a large meal. In infants, there is often no delay between the onset of feeding and the gastrocolic reflex, which explains why many babies have bowel movements during feedings.

The rectal contractions caused by the gastrocolic reflex can cause the cramping I've just mentioned. Usually the cramping is fleeting, lasting at most one or two minutes. It's during this period that the baby may cry.

Some parents, confused by the crying, will stop the feeding and not resume until they have gotten a burp from the baby, ascribing the crying to gas. But when the cramp passes on its own, without the benefit of a burp, the baby will want to start feeding again, and the cry will now signify hunger. Note, by the way, that infants will not cry in the middle of a feeding because they need to burp. Burping is another of those cultural catch-alls used to explain babies' cries. I discuss this topic in detail later in the chapter, but it's worth noting here that as a cause of crying in infants, the need for burping is highly over-rated.

Some parents might interpret crying in the middle of feeding to mean that the baby is full and no longer wants to feed. But again, as soon as the slight cramp passes, this baby might be eager to get back to feeding and will become agitated if kept from the breast or bottle.

If your baby cries out in the middle of a feeding and you are not sure of the cause, I recommend that you do the following:

1. Stop the feeding and hold the infant for a couple of minutes to allow time for the cramping to stop.

2. When the crying stops within a couple of minutes, resume feeding.

If the crying was the result of the gastrocolic reflex, the baby will happily start to feed again, but if the cry has some other meaning, the baby will continue to cry. In that case, follow the steps in the program described in Chapter 5.

It is important for you to remember that the gastro-colic reflex is *never* associated with diarrhea or vomit-ing. If these symptoms develop during a feeding, call your baby's doctor. They are symptoms of illness, though in all probability mild illness, and are not indicators of the gastrocolic reflex or infant colic syndrome.

To summarize this lengthy section on the relation-ship between infant crying and the need for food, you can end or prevent bouts of infant colic syndrome re-lated to hunger by following these steps:

- Feed your baby on demand.

- Wait until your baby is six months old before add-ing solid food to the diet of formula or breast milk.

- Always consider hunger a possible reason for cry-ing, but never force the baby to feed.

- By following the first three steps, rest assured that you are doing everything possible to enable the baby to regulate food intake naturally and are therefore doing everything possible to control obesity.

- Have your baby's weight gain checked frequently at well-baby checks.

- Be aware that babies sometimes cry in the middle

of a feeding because of discomfort stemming from the gastrocolic reflex.

CRYING AND THE NEED FOR SLEEP

The amount of sleep infants need varies greatly among individuals. Again, it doesn't hurt to remember that in trying to understand our babies, we're second-guessing individuals with their own temperaments and idiosyncrasies just as distinctive as those among adults. Reminding ourselves of this fact can help us resist the temptation to focus solely on norms.

Still, the norms are useful to describe generalities, which have their place in a discussion like this. Six-week-old infants, *on the average*, sleep fifteen hours a day, though some need as few as twelve hours of sleep in every twenty-four and some need as many as eighteen.

Infants also vary in how easily they fall asleep. Some seem to fall asleep effortlessly wherever they are the moment they become tired, while others have a lot of trouble falling asleep, especially when they are tired. All such variations amount to individual preferences. Our job as parents is to discern the preferences of our own babies. As in the realm of feeding, there are many myths and misconceptions about the amount of sleep a child of a certain age should have every day. The following section calls your attention to these myths and misconceptions so you can recognize them, identify them for what they are, and resist the temptation to believe them.

Myths and Misconceptions Regarding Sleep Schedules

Many people, including many doctors, believe that infants should have a daily routine in which the number of sleeping hours remains stable. For them, *regularity* is key, and sometimes becomes more important the further from a regular schedule the baby gets. The argument is that such routines should be arranged to be convenient for the parents. And again, the less the baby's and parents' schedules coincide, the more these believers invoke the need for imposing some order. That call for order in the midst of a growing *disorder* can add more confusion to a situation.

You should not be surprised when I say that the first step toward reducing the confusion is to throw out the schedule and start acting on the baby's individual desires and need for sleep. Trying to ignore the baby's temperament is like setting up your picnic on the slope of a volcano. Maybe the volcano won't erupt and your plans will work out. But maybe it will erupt, and that will be the end of your picnic. Maybe your baby will go to sleep during the times you considered appropriate and convenient; in that case your schedule will seem workable. But maybe the baby will refuse to go to sleep or will wake up long before expected, despite your well-laid plans.

As with feeding patterns, it is the infant's temperament that determines his or her sleeping pattern, and not your will, hopes, or parenting skills. If your baby is a person with an easygoing, flexible temperament, it may indeed be possible to put him or her to bed at the time you choose, and a baby inclined toward regularity may even slide into the routine with no effort. But if you have a determined and tenacious infant, getting that child to bed at the time you choose may be quite difficult indeed, and you'll probably manage it only at the expense of a great deal of crying.

Linda, for example, noticed that her baby, Judy, woke every morning at ten on the dot, took several long naps during the day, and went to sleep every night at midnight. Linda herself longed to go to bed earlier—at about ten-thirty each night—and hoped to accustom Judy to an earlier bedtime by waking her at eight in the morning and laying her down in her crib at eight-thirty at night.

Few infants would take easily to these changes, and Judy was not one of them. When Linda awakened her at eight in the morning, she cried for a long time, inter-rupting the early-morning breakfast routine of parents and siblings. And despite Linda's attempts to cut down on Judy's nap time so she might become tired earlier for the night, she was never able to get Judy used to the eight-thirty bedtime. The result of the struggle against Judy's particular sleep needs was a baby who cried a great deal throughout the day because she wanted to be asleep and who cried a great deal at the end of the day because she wanted to remain awake.

My Baby's Not Sleeping Enough

The amount of sleep an infant needs varies from in-fant to infant and the range is quite wide. In general, full term babies will sleep anywhere from twelve hours a day to eighteen hours a day.

There's no denying that having a young infant with very low sleep needs—say twelve hours every twenty-four—can be extremely trying, since wakeful infants need constant attention. Nevertheless, it is not at all abnor-mal for a child to sleep only twelve hours a day. I have talked with many parents who have worried that their babies were hyperactive because they remained awake when other babies of their age took long naps or slept through the night. But wakefulness in a baby is merely an individual characteristic, not a medical condition.

Trying to force a baby who is not tired to sleep is an effort in vain. The baby will simply cry to be picked up and, if left to cry for too long, will eventually become so agitated that he or she will cry even *after* being picked up. Most parents find it more unpleasant to listen to a baby crying than to attend to the demands of a wakeful but satisfied baby.

Individual Sleep Habits

How do we know when babies become tired? Some fall asleep spontaneously when tired, but others become fussy and irritable. In my experience, many parents, especially first-time parents, expect the tired baby to fall asleep quietly and must learn that crying and fussing can also be signs of tiredness.

It's safe to say that most of us have been around groups of people in which exhausted young children have been allowed to spin more and more out of control. Any number of Thanksgivings come to my mind. The parents of these children, apparently unaware that "hyper" behavior can signal a need for sleep, let the children "enjoy themselves." It is true that in general, tired adults slow down gradually until they put themselves to bed (though most of us have experienced the condition of being unable to sleep because we were "overtired"), but in children, the activity level sometimes speeds up as they grow more and more tired. In infants, the analogy to this speeding up can be fussiness and crying.

What is the appropriate response when you suspect your infant's crying is due to tiredness? Some parents walk with the infant until he or she falls off to sleep and then lay the baby down in the crib. I would advise against this approach for two reasons. First, many infants find walking and rocking *stimulating*, rather than sleep-inducing, and the motion prevents them from falling asleep. Second, if walking and rocking does help the baby fall asleep, you may be creating a ritual you'll wish you hadn't started, one that will be very difficult to break as the child becomes older.

When your infant shows signs of tiredness, try to avoid any unnecessary ritual and simply put the baby down in the crib to sleep. If he or she begins to cry, pay careful attention to the quality of the cry and how long it lasts. Some infants always cry for a few minutes before falling off to sleep, and the quality of this cry is usually quite characteristic. The cry starts off loud but becomes quieter and quieter, then stops and starts again. This pattern continues for a few minutes until the baby is finally asleep. If you misinterpret the cry to mean that the infant is not tired and therefore pick him or her up, the baby will become agitated and begin to cry inconsolably. On the other hand, if after being placed in the crib the infant cries more and more loudly without interruption, your suspicions that the infant was tired will have been proven wrong. You have a wide-awake baby on your hands, and there's no point in leaving this baby in the bed. If you leave the baby to cry, he or she will become agitated and will continue to cry for a long time.

It is also not uncommon for babies to cry while asleep. It is assumed that this happens at a time in the sleep cycle when the adult would be dreaming. It's easy to misinterpret such a cry, as a signal that the baby is awake and wants to be picked up, but if you pick up a baby in response to this cry you'll soon be holding a crying, unhappy infant.

Babies also wake temporarily and cry for a minute or two before falling back to sleep. This seems to happen during the period in the sleep cycle known as "light sleep." In adults, this is the phase when we awaken, adjust our pillows, and then quickly fall back to sleep. It is easy to misinterpret this cry and assume that the baby is finished sleeping, especially if the infant is sleeping close by.

To avoid misinterpreting such cries and interrupting the baby's sleep, listen to the cries for several minutes. If the infant is awake and signaling to be picked up, then the cry will quickly become loud and constant. If the infant is asleep and crying out momentarily, the cry will soften and stop.

Parents sometimes tell me they mistakenly wake their infants from sleep. In these cases, the baby is usually sleeping in the parents' room and the solution, of course, is to move the baby into another room for sleeping. Yet, many parents derive a sense of security from having the baby in the same room with them. The need to be close by seems natural to me and I see no reason to discourage parents from sleeping in the same room with their infant. The arrangement can have its own disadvantages, though, when the parents are light sleepers and awaken every time the infant sighs, coughs, moves in the crib, or cries during sleep. When this is the case, it is better for all concerned to have the baby sleep in a separate room.

Sleeping Through the Night

Understandably, most parents look forward to the day when their baby begins to sleep through the night. Infants have a natural diurnal sleep pattern—that is, they naturally sleep more during the night than during the day. However, in many babies this pattern does not establish itself immediately, but takes several weeks to become set. Like all other diurnal animals, the infant is affected by the rhythm of sunset and sunrise. To match this pattern and encourage night sleeping, in the daytime have the baby sleep in a light, airy, somewhat noisy room, and in the nighttime put the baby down in a dark, quiet room. Also, watch your infant to determine whether he or she is more comfortable in a small, enclosed space such as a cradle or a roomier area such as a crib. If the baby shows a preference, by all means honor it.

Still at this point the baby will probably be far from sleeping straight through the night. He or she will most likely be waking once or twice a night for feeding. How soon the middle-of-the-night feeding disappears depends on three factors:

- The feeding method

- The infant's size

- The baby's temperament

Studies have shown that breast-fed babies normally wake more often in the night than bottle-fed babies. In fact, some breast-fed babies never start sleeping through the night spontaneously, and those that do usually begin to sleep through the night at an older age than bottle-fed babies. For example, a bottle-fed infant with a birth weight of more than seven pounds will usually sleep eight hours a night by eight weeks of age. A breast-fed baby with the same birth weight will usually begin this sleeping pattern by ten weeks of age.

Infants cannot sleep through the night until they are large enough to endure a fast of eight to eleven hours in length. This varies somewhat from infant to infant, but as a rule of thumb, an infant who weighs more than nine pounds can sleep for eight hours without awakening for food.

As for the all-pervasive last factor, infant temperament, this takes precedence over any other rule of thumb. A ten-pound baby might prefer to take small, frequent feedings during the night, contrary to the predicted eight-hour pattern of sleep. If you try to insist that your infant stop the middle-of-the-night feeding before he or she is ready, you will be letting yourself in for a night filled with crying.

What if your infant is ten to twelve weeks old, weighs ten pounds, and is still waking up at night to feed? This child is unlikely to begin sleeping through the night spontaneously, and it is appropriate to look into the issue further by speaking with your physician.

CRYING AND THE NEED TO SUCK

Infants are born with a desire to suck that is independent of their need for calories and nutrition. And when a baby wants something to suck on, which happens even when he or she is not hungry, that baby will cry, sending you the message that the need is unmet. Often this occurs at the end of a feeding, when the baby has taken in all the breast milk or formula he or she needs but wants to continue to suck.

The act of sucking is both pleasurable and soothing for the infant and has a pacifying effect. In primitive cultures where mothers go bare-breasted, they often put the infant to the empty breast as a calming technique. During nursing, infants take in 90 percent of the calories contained in the breast within the first five to ten minutes of a feeding, yet many infants will nurse for twenty to twenty-five minutes on each breast, simply enjoying the process of sucking, without receiving milk.

The pacifier is the modern substitute for the empty breast. But please note: Pacifiers were invented to meet the sucking need. Sucking did *not* develop in response to the existence of pacifiers. The point might seem minor until you have had occasion to ponder the pacifier "problem." The pacifier has probably been a source of controversy since the first care-giver gave a crying infant a finger to suck!

The Pacifier "Problem"

Consider Carl, Marie, and their four-month-old, Lily. Lily was an active sucker, and at each feeding continued to nurse long after the breast was dry, sometimes as long as half an hour on a side. When Marie took her off before she had satisfied her urge to suck, she cried inconsolably. But Marie was a busy woman with work as well as other children to attend to, and in desperation she bought an array of pacifiers. She was delighted to find that Lily easily took the first one she tried, greatly freeing up Marie's time.

But whenever Carl came home to find the pacifier in Lily's mouth, he uttered a snort of disgust and plucked it out, leaving Lily to stare in silent surprise for a few seconds and then to protest loudly while a soon-familiar argument went on between her parents. Note that this scenario usually took place at about six o'clock, when Marie was busy preparing dinner and the two other children in the family were alternately asking when dinner would be ready and asking for help with their homework. Carl's response was to ignore the commotion and become engrossed in the television news. And Lily would cry on, while Marie juggled pots and pans and the baby swing, all the while calling out to Carl, "For heaven's sake, Carl, let's have some peace and quiet. The pacifier, *please!*"

"No child of mine is going to go around sucking on a piece of rubber," was Carl's position. "It looks bad and it *is* bad—it'll spoil her personality and giver her an over-bite besides."

In exasperation, Marie would sneak the pacifier back into Lily's mouth only to have Carl explode the next time he passed through the kitchen. This is a very common scene. For many people, the sight of the pacifier in a baby's mouth seems to blind them to the object's practical value. Often those who protest the use of the pacifier object that it is an "artificial" way to calm a crying baby and conveys the idea that the parent is using a "trick" rather than dealing with the baby in some more "authentic" way. For this reason, many parents who would otherwise make use of a pacifier feel guilty about it and so forego this simple way of meeting the infant's need to suck.

Like most prejudices, this prejudice against pacifiers is based on misinformation. Pacifiers have no negative effects. And they simply and quickly meet the infant's normal physiological need to suck. The only determining factor is whether or not the baby will take the pacifier and use it to satisfy the sucking need.

There are, of course, guidelines to using the pacifier with safety. Above all, never tie the pacifier on a string and loop it like a necklace around the baby's neck. Also, only buy pacifiers that are made as one piece so they can't come apart into swallowable pieces. Finally, avoid the makeshift pacifier—the bottle nipple plugged with cotton. There have been reports of babies aspirating the nipple when such contraptions come apart.

The Thumbsucking "Problem"

Some babies learn early to satisfy their sucking needs themselves by sucking their thumbs. Usually finding the thumb and using it this way is a happy accident that becomes a habit—but it is not until the baby is about three months of age that she will be able to purposefully place her thumb in her mouth for sucking.

Thumbsucking, of course, has long been surrounded by its own stormy controversy. If your infant sucks his or her thumb, you probably hear the following comments or versions of them on the average of once or twice a week:

- "You really ought to break him of that habit now or he's still going to be sucking his thumb in the third grade."

- "Oh, boy. You're in for a big orthodontics bill. Don't you know thumbsucking causes overbite?"

- "That baby's already sucking her thumb. Must be an awfully needy baby."

- "Just pull her thumb out of her mouth every time she puts it in. She'll soon learn not to do it."

- "You should use what my mom used on *my* thumb when I was a baby. Some foul-tasting stuff, but it worked. I used it on all my kids."

The fact is that in children under one year of age, thumbsucking, like sucking the pacifier, serves a normal physiological purpose: It fulfills the need to suck beyond feeding. After one year of age, thumbsucking serves the same function as the attachment to objects such as a blanket or teddy bear that the baby carries everywhere. It provides familiarity. Most children who suck their thumbs stop by age two. In those few instances in which thumbsucking persists beyond that age, there are still several years to go before the habit can cause permanent teeth-placement problems—about five years of age.

A good way to view it is to think of thumbs as built-in pacifiers. Parents who don't count themselves lucky if their babies manage to use their thumbs to pacify themselves are missing a great chance to simplify their care-taking system. With the thumb in use, there's one fewer thing, the pacifier, to keep track of and bring along with you when you leave the house.

On the negative side, though, we have much less control over stopping thumbsucking than we do over using a pacifier. The latter can be taken away and, after a short mourning period, forgotten. Thumbsucking is harder to control and should be stopped by age five, when teeth placement can be permanently affected.

Trying to stop a young infant from thumbsucking is next to impossible and is only accomplished with a great deal of crying. However, after the child reaches two years of age, parents can be effective in ending the habit by using behavior modification—that is, by rewarding the child for not sucking the thumb.

If you haven't given thought to sucking as a fundamental need and permit neither thumbsucking nor a pacifier, you may be contending with a "colicky" baby if your baby has a strong sucking need—either that or your baby is spending long sessions nursing at an empty breast. Families have come to me complaining of colic and been unaware of the fundamental need to suck. Often, their babies are crying four or five hours a day despite all efforts to console them. When I put these families on my program and encourage them to try a pacifier along with the other need-satisfying options, the excessive crying disappears.

Individual Variations

As with all the other fundamental needs, the strength of the need to suck varies from baby to baby. Some infants appear to fulfill this need while feeding, while others want to suck all the time. The only way to find out how much sucking your infant wants is to offer the pacifier whenever your baby cries. If the infant is crying to communicate a need other than that of sucking, he or she will refuse the pacifier and continue to cry.

Breast-Feeding and the Need to Suck

No one would offer a baby an empty bottle to suck on, but as I have suggested, offering an empty breast is indeed an appropriate response to the infant's need to suck.

Still, in its dual function as source of nourishment and "nature's pacifier," the breast can pose special problems when you are trying to interpret your infant's cries. It is not uncommon for a breast-fed infant who needs to suck to refuse a pacifier and to cry until he or she is offered the empty breast. The reason for this is that many breast-fed babies find the texture of the artificial nipple on a pacifier unpleasant. (These are usually the same infants who refuse a supplemental bottle.)

In addition, for many breast-fed babies, being held and cuddled is associated with being nursed. They will refuse the pacifier and will not be happy simply being held without being given the breast. This situation can be extremely trying for the mother, who is generally seeking a way to cut down on the time spent nursing the baby so she can attend to her other responsibilities. If the child must be nursed not only to satisfy hunger but also to satisfy the sucking and holding needs, it is likely that the mother will be immobilized for a good many hours a day.

This is a problem for which there are no quick and easy solutions. One recommendation is to try to head off the situation before it develops by beginning to offer the pacifier very early in the infant's life—within the first two to three weeks. Try to get your baby used to the texture and consistency of the artificial nipple so he or she will associate it with something familiar and comforting. This also applies, by the way, if you are planning to incorporate bottle-feeding into your baby care plan—the pacifier nipple will help familiarize your baby with the texture of an artificial nipple.

A second recommendation is for the father or other care-giver to hold the baby and offer the pacifier. The infant quickly comes to associate the nursing mother with breast milk and the natural nipple. Taking an artificial nipple from her may come as a shock and a disappointment, whereas the same association does not apply to the father or other care-giver. Again, the earlier you start this the better.

To sum up, in your effort to interpret your baby's cries and make the appropriate response, be sure to consider the need to suck, a need often overlooked in the scramble to soothe the crying baby. A pacifier, a thumb, or an empty breast will do wonders when the baby is in need of calming himself by sucking.

CRYING AND THE NEED TO BE HELD

The fourth fundamental need of infants, and another that may be unconsciously overlooked when the baby has become agitated, is the simple need to be held. When babies are trying to convey this need to their parents by crying, simply picking them up, sitting with them in a chair, and holding them close puts an end to the crying.

This need for proximity with an adult is not a simple expression of "loneliness," but rather, as experts agree, a need favored by evolution. In prehistoric times, infants near their parents were protected from predators; those left alone were unprotected and at risk.

During the 1940s, studies of infants raised in English orphanages revealed that these children grew slowly compared with children in families, and were slow in reaching their developmental milestones such as walking and talking. Further investigation revealed that the care-givers of these children spent little if any time holding, cuddling, and physically comforting them, and that it was the lack of such physical nurturing that was responsible for the children's slow development. We now accept as scientific fact a notion that makes sense to most of us intuitively: Without comforting and reassuring physical contact from adults, babies fail to thrive.

Still, as with the other needs we have discussed, the actual amount of holding and touching infants need varies greatly among individuals. Some babies require relatively little holding while others always seem unhappy unless they are in someone's arms. Where this is the case, that old bugaboo "spoiling" enters the picture—remember those old government pamphlets that warned against creating a "household tyrant." Parents are often afraid that "giving in to the baby's demands" by picking him or her up when crying shows a weakness in their character and also threatens to weaken the baby's character. Myth and misconception surface again—the result of well-meaning friends and relatives with their own ideas lifting an eyebrow or exchanging glances when they see a concerned parent unhesitatingly pick up a crying child.

The Question of "Spoiling"

I want to return to this question of "spoiling" as it relates to infants and lay it to rest once and for all. What do people mean when they say one is spoiling a baby? Usually that the parents are allowing the baby to "manipulate" them—that is, by hook or crook to get them to meet his or her demands.

Parents who fear that they are falling into this "trap" are generally thinking about the future and imagining that the pattern set in early infancy will remain throughout adulthood. They worry that if they pick up the child every time he or she cries, they'll eventually be buying candy and toys whenever the child raises a fuss: "I'm not going to allow a child to run my life. Best to show him who's boss, set the house limits right off the bat. There will be no manipulation going on around here."

Setting limits is unquestionably an important function of parenting. Children need to learn that they certainly cannot have anything they want, and the more consistent the limit-setting, the more clearly children understand the bounds of good behavior. But the learning of limits *cannot take place during the early months of life.* Infants do not have the cognitive, or thinking, skills either to manipulate the parents or to understand rules of behavior. The idea that the child should begin to learn "how we do things around here" at the age of one, two, three, or four months is inappropriate.

Also inappropriate is the language often used to describe this "spoiling" process. The word *manipulate* connotes a kind of guile that is absent in the young baby.

And the word *demand*—as in "he's manipulating you to get you to meet his demands"—is meaningless when applied to a being whose survival depends on adults to meet his or her built-in physiological and psychological needs. The word *communicating* is appropriate here; *manipulating* is not. *Needs*, yes; *demands*, no. Finally, *nurturing*, yes. But *spoiling?* Never. It is impossible to "spoil" a young infant.

Beyond meeting the basic needs that keep the child healthy and thriving, the main parenting task during infancy is to foster a sense of security in the baby. You do this by responding to your baby's needs, showing the baby that his or her environment does indeed respond.

Choosing not to pick up a baby who wants to be held, letting that baby cry, will not teach the baby to withhold her cries. Infants are *incapable* of learning to suppress their needs. Rather, failing to respond to such cries will only make the baby insecure, which in turn will *increase* the desire to be held. But holding the baby whenever she cries to be held will result in *diminishing* the baby's need to be held as the child's sense of security within a responsive environment grows.

"Walking" the Baby

It is important that you do not interpret the need to be held as a need to be walked—that is, carried back and forth on endless trips around the house. An adult satisfies the baby's need to be held simply by sitting in a chair and holding the baby quietly. If the baby stops crying when you hold him quietly in this way, then the crying was expressing the need to be held. If, to stop the infant's cries, you must get up and walk the child, then the need for holding was not the message behind the crying. Walking may stop the baby temporarily from signaling the specific need that *is* expressed in the cries, but only by distracting the infant for a time, after which crying will resume.

Charles and Karen, a professional couple in their mid-thirties, came to me exhausted from carrying their baby, Terry, around the house half the night. On warm nights, Charles even carried the baby to town in a baby carrier. They had been doing this since Terry's birth on the advice of Karen's parents, for whom "walking the baby" was the magical cure for everything.

"Why not just sit with the baby?" I suggested. "That's all she needs."

Relief! Charles and Karen may not have started getting much more sleep, for Terry needed a lot of holding. But at least they were off their feet. Terry's excessive crying had prohibited them from even considering a less aggressive mode of meeting her need to be held. Once again, in the midst of infant colic syndrome, well-meaning but not necessarily accurate advice confused the issue.

Putting the Sleeping Baby Down

Glenda, single working mother of three-month-old Gloria, came to the office frazzled and exhausted. "She just won't let me put her down. She's quiet as long as I hold her and eventually drifts off in my arms, but no matter how exhausted she is, as soon as she finds herself in the crib she's yelling bloody murder. I pick her up, she goes to sleep. I put her down, she wakes up. Sometimes we go through that cycle as many as eight or ten times in a night. I'm a walking wreck."

Parents often describe this situation and wonder how to handle it. The baby falls asleep easily but invariably wakes upon being placed in the crib. I look at this problem as a natural consequence of the baby's desire to be held. In the parents' arms, the infant feels warm and secure. Consequently, he falls asleep easily. But once in the crib, the baby quickly realizes that the sense of security and proximity to the parent has ended—and begins to cry, expressing the need to be held.

Some babies will fall back to sleep even after crying for several minutes. But others are in for the duration—they will cry until they are picked up. Simply letting these more tenacious babies cry is never effective. But what is one to do if not spend day and night sitting in a chair and holding the baby?

If you have a tenacious baby with a strong need to be held, I recommend that you focus much of your attention on *not* waking the baby when you place him or her in the crib. Try with all your ingenuity not to convey the fact that the transfer has occurred. Here are some hints:

- To avoid a change of temperature, warm the crib with a heating pad before putting the baby down. (*Note: Be sure to remove the pad before placing the infant in the crib*, and check carefully to make sure the crib is not too hot.)

- Wait until the baby appears to be in a *deep sleep* before putting him or her down.

- Since changes in position from somewhat vertical to horizontal are strong signals to the body, change the baby's position very slowly, in stages.

By focusing on the task at hand and practicing, you will soon learn to make the transfer to the crib without waking the baby. In the meantime, if the baby does wake and cry, pick him or her up before agitation develops and try again.

CRYING AND THE NEED FOR STIMULATION

Babies get bored! It's a fact. From birth onward, human beings need visual and aural stimulation—that is, stimulation of the senses of vision and hearing. Our normal neurological and emotional development depends on it. Infants in need of stimulation will cry for it. So if your baby has been fed and is not tired, is disinterested in the pacifier or the breast, and squirms and cries when held quietly, the cries may be signaling the fifth infant need—the need for stimulation.

It is a widespread notion that infants can become overstimulated by "too much attention." A baby who is receptive to stimulation cannot be stimulated too much. But what is usually referred to as overstimulation is the stimulating of a baby who is not ready for it. This is avoided when we match our responses to the baby's specific needs. But it is rare indeed to hear a lay person acknowledge that an infant is in need of something to listen to or something to see, and yet these needs are very real.

Kinds of Stimulation

The last thing I am suggesting, of course, is that you strap your three-month-old baby into a tiny Walkman and play tapes of classical music or French lessons. In the first few months of life, the stimulation given to a baby need not be complicated. Simply putting the baby in an infant seat in a room where there is lots of activity is often enough. The movement and noises people make as they go about the house are just what the baby needs. Talking to the baby, too, meets the stimulation needs and, at the appropriate time, begins to fill the baby's head with language, a prerequisite for learning to talk.

While paying attention to the baby's stimulation needs, be aware that during the first eight to ten weeks after birth, the attention span is short. Therefore, the baby might tire after ten or fifteen minutes at the heart of the household. So don't be surprised if the baby seems happy for this time period and then begins to cry—this time, perhaps, out of the need for sleep. Fifteen minutes may be all the stimulation he or she can take in at this time.

In considering the kinds of stimulation appropriate for infants less than three months old, it is important to know just where they are developmentally. For example, at birth, babies can barely focus their eyes at all. They can see large, extremely bright, and moving objects, but they are unable to see faces well enough to distinguish one from another. At one month of age, they can't see clearly beyond 12 inches. By three months of age, they can see a toy several feet away. At birth, they can hear but are scared by loud noises. It is not until several weeks after birth that babies show any evidence of recognizing the human voice.

You can see, then, that most mobiles would serve little purpose in entertaining the young infant. Mobiles move and are colorful, but babies probably don't notice them unless they are fairly large. Toys of any sort are not much use before three months, but large, bright, moving objects—people moving around a room, for instance—would certainly capture the infant's interest. Babies do hear and appear to enjoy music, so a musical mobile or other sources of music would offer aural stimulation even in the early weeks. But the noise of dinner preparations in a busy family would probably be as captivating at this stage. Wind-up swings with their steady motion are also pleasing to most infants.

Individual Variations

The need for stimulation varies enormously. Some babies spend long periods awake, alert, and receptive to stimulation. These are often the same babies who require relatively little sleep—those who can sit in an infant seat on the kitchen counter and quite happily watch you attend to your tasks or a meal. Others, as I've suggested earlier, tire quickly from such exposure and need to be held, or to go to sleep, or to engage in sucking.

As you begin to sense the level of stimulation your child requires and enjoys, try not to compare him or her with the "norms" for babies of the same age, for the range of variation is tremendous. Instead, here again is an opportunity to sense something about your baby's personal uniqueness—the qualities that make your baby an individual.

BUT WHAT ABOUT...?

You'll notice that this list of the five reasons why healthy babies cry—the needs for food, sleep, sucking, being held, and stimulation—does not include many other reasons commonly cited for infant crying. Teething is conspicuous in its absence; so is the need to burp, or "bubble." And so is the need for a diaper change or the feeding of water to the baby. I haven't overlooked these reasons; they simply don't qualify as factors in why healthy babies cry.

Teething

Teething pain—discomfort associated with the eruption of teeth through the gums—does not really apply to babies in the first three months of life. The average age for the first tooth to appear is six months, and a tooth is rarely seen before three months. Still, babies begin to drool excessively and to gum objects at three months of age. Parents often associate this behavior with teething, but it really has nothing to do with it. Drooling and gumming objects are normal developmental behaviors that appear as the infant grows. They occur at three months whether the infant's first tooth appears then, at six months, or at ten months of age. Doctors and parents are always arguing about what behaviors teething causes or doesn't cause in the child. Fortunately, we need not concern ourselves with it except to assert that teething is not a matter of concern in very young infants.

Diaper Changes

Do babies cry because of the discomfort of a soiled diaper? This is another unnecessary question, made so by the fact that babies always need their diapers changed. Diaper changes are essential for skin care in the diaper area. If soiled diapers are left on the baby, the skin will become inflamed, then ulcerated, and finally infected. I believe it would insult my readers' intelligence to remind them to change the baby's diaper, since changing the baby whenever the need arises is essential. It is true that some toddlers will walk around for hours with a wet or dirty diaper without asking for it to be changed, while others will ask their parents to change them immediately. This variation in skin sensitivity probably exists in infants, too. Some infants will cry from discomfort when their diapers are soiled, and others will not. However, the question is academic in the face of hygiene and good skin care.

Burping

Air swallowed during feeding will escape whether a baby is consciously "burped" or not. The infant's esophagus is immature and not only will it not hold in air but it doesn't ever do a good job of keeping down milk, which accounts for the frequency of spitting up in babies. If a baby is not formally burped and still retains air in the stomach, the worst that will happen is that the gas will escape while the infant is lying in the crib; at that time some milk will probably be regurgitated along with the air.

I have never seen a baby cry because of not being burped, though I have seen babies crying because they were burped too frequently. Consider the story of Alice.

Mary brought her infant daughter, Alice, in to see me because the baby cried a great deal with every feeding. When I reviewed Mary's feeding technique with her, I learned that she was interrupting the feeding after every ounce in order to get Alice to burp. It took Mary five to ten minutes to get Alice to burp. She wouldn't continue until she did, and meanwhile Alice was crying a good deal. The entire four-ounce feeding routinely took at least an hour and was pure hell. This feeding approach, taught to Mary by her mother, was intended to prevent the baby from getting gas and then colic.

What exactly was happening here? Whether or not a baby burps depends entirely on how much air is swallowed during the feeding. Some babies swallow no air and besides not *needing* to burp after a meal, simply *cannot* burp then. Other babies swallow a great deal of air and will burp freely after a feeding. In Alice's case, after only one ounce of formula, she had swallowed no air and couldn't have burped for the life of her. But she was hungry and cried to be fed, and after crying for ten minutes *had* swallowed a lot of air and *could* finally burp. This would make Mary happy and resume feeding, only to begin the cycle all over again after the next ounce.

Some parents interrupt the feeding after one or two ounces because their babies frequently spit up milk. It is common for doctors to advise parents to burp such babies frequently—and, again, the interruption in feeding results in much infant crying. But spitting up in babies has nothing to do with gas. Rather, it is related to the immaturity of the esophagus, the tube of muscle that transmits food from mouth to stomach.

My advice is to stop *once* in the middle of a feeding and gently burp the baby for a minute or so. If the baby doesn't burp, don't worry; simply resume feeding. Spend a minute or so burping the baby at the end of the feeding, too. Again, if the baby doesn't burp, simply stop and don't worry.

Offering Water

Babies don't need water, and rarely cry for it. Normally, babies don't get thirsty independently of becoming hungry—the two needs occur simultaneously.

There is ample water content in formula, as you well know if you use it in concentrated form—you prepare it by mixing in one part water to one part formula. Breast milk, too, contains ample water.

However, if it is ninety-five degrees outside, the humidity is 100 percent, you have no air conditioning, and your fan is broken, your baby may indeed feel thirsty, and you can give him or her water. Otherwise, babies who want fluids are hungry, so give formula or breast milk, not water.

Things Parents Do

You'll notice that many of the things that people frequently do to make babies stop crying are also absent from this discussion—taking the infant for a car ride, or even placing the baby on top of a running clothes dryer. It is true that in some babies these maneuvers may quell crying—if not in all circumstances, then in some. But these are all *temporary* measures that distract the baby from the need she is really communicating. The distractions may temporarily soothe the baby but do not ultimately solve the problem.

The objective in this chapter has been to clarify what is often an extremely confused area of family life—why healthy babies cry. Simply knowing the possible reasons for your baby's cries, as well as recognizing myths and misconceptions so you don't waste time chasing false leads, means that you are halfway home in solving the riddle of why your baby is crying.

The second and last lap in interpreting your baby's cries and in curing or preventing colic involves a quick, orderly trial-and-error approach supplemented by careful record keeping that clarifies *your* baby's unique, individual messages. In this chapter, we have dealt with all healthy babies and the generalizations that can be made about why they cry. In the next chapter, we turn to the particulars: your baby, your household, and the specific messages in your infant's cries.

Chapter 5
Responding to Your Baby's Cry: The Program

The purpose of this chapter is to translate the counseling I do with families of colicky babies into a program you can follow at home in accurately determining the meaning of and response to your baby's cries.

Key words to keep in mind here are *clarity* and *order*—these are the qualities the program brings to the problem of infant colic syndrome. A third key element is *quick action*. In essence, the program leads you through a quick trial-and-error search for the right response.

Who will benefit from the program? Families with babies who have infant colic syndrome will see a dramatic improvement—usually within two to three days. Improvement may take longer if the problem has persisted for months. The program is also helpful to those parents who want to see their baby's cries reduced even if the baby's crying already falls into the "normal" thirty-to ninety-minute range.

It should help to emphasize at the outset that this program really works—and it works quickly—within seven minutes to stop an episode of crying. It has helped countless parents in my medical practice, and I have also shown it to be true by means of two empirically designed and controlled studies. Earlier, I mentioned these studies in reference to the question of whether changes in formula for bottle-fed babies had a positive effect in reducing colic. Here, I will describe one of the studies again to reassure you about the effectiveness of the program.

In one study, I compared the effects of two colic treatments: changing infant formula and counseling parents in responding to their babies' cries as communication. Both groups of babies studied were crying at least three hours a day at the start of the study. Infants given a new formula did show a slow decrease in crying over nine days. However, by the ninth day, these infants were still crying an average of two hours a day—still substantially in excess of the normal range of thirty to ninety minutes per twenty-four hours. In contrast, those infants whose parents were counseled to respond to their cries as communication were crying on an average of ninety minutes a day, the outside limit of the normal range, within three days. And at the end of nine days, those same babies were crying only sixty minutes a day, well within the normal range for babies of their age.

The program of counseling that I used with these parents and that is translated here into a quick and orderly trial-and-error system is made up of four parts.

PART A: VISITING THE DOCTOR

I have already covered Part A comprehensively: having your infant's complete medical history taken and a physical examination performed by a physician whom you trust and with whom you can communicate easily. The doctor will weigh and measure the baby carefully to ascertain that the weight gain and linear growth are normal. Next, the doctor will look for possible causes of pain; it is rare for a doctor to find problems that the parents are completely unaware of, but it is possible. Thus, the doctor will make sure your baby has no such problems as chronic ear infections, an incarcerated inguinal hernia, or severe nasal congestion. All these not only require medical attention but cause pain or discomfort that could account for prolonged crying.

Further, the doctor should do a rectal exam to make sure the infant does not have a narrowed anal canal, a condition that could cause discomfort with bowel movements. Hard stools can also be painful and could result in an inconsolably crying infant, so the doctor should question you in detail about the consistency of the baby's stools. Other possible causes of pain to be ruled out include a fractured clavicle, or collarbone, sustained during birth (this is not a common occurrence, but it does happen and can be overlooked), ingrown and infected toenails, and a hair wrapped tightly around the infant's toes (another rare finding).

When the physician takes the medical history, make sure to mention any vomiting and/or diarrhea. As I have made clear, these symptoms rule out infant colic syndrome and suggest a gastrointestinal problem needing immediate attention that could account for the baby's crying.

Once the doctor has determined that your child is *completely healthy,* you are ready to proceed to Part B.

One final note: After you familiarize yourself with the program, be sure to read the case histories at the end of this chapter. These stories, drawn from my patient files, show the kinds of responses I suggest parents try after I analyze the behavior diaries they keep on their babies. The specific circumstances and responses described could spark an insight into your own situation. The case histories should also have the effect of further reassuring you that your baby's crying will soon diminish as you grapple with the *source* rather than the effects of infant colic syndrome.

PART B: KEEPING A BEHAVIOR DIARY

Basic to the goal of clarity is the behavior diary, or daily journal, in which you will precisely record all your baby's behavior—sleeping, waking, crying, happy time, and so on. One of the nearly immediate benefits of the diary will be to let you know just exactly how much time your baby is crying. At the end of the first twenty-four hours, you may find that the journal has confirmed your estimate. But chances are the opposite will be true—you will find that you inadvertently exaggerated the actual number of minutes your baby has been crying each day. The anxiety, exhaustion, and confusion that so often surround infant colic syndrome can intensify the experience to such a degree that parents often overestimate their child's actual crying time, frequently by one and a half times the actual amount.

Refer now to the section of blank diary pages at the back of this book. Two of the forms will be used for your initial assessment, giving you a twenty-four-hour description of the circumstances before you begin the program. In addition, to allow room for errors in record keeping and to cover all contingencies, including the unusual cases, in which colic takes longer to abate, I have provided blanks for seven twenty-four-hour cycles.

The blank forms are designed to be as easy as possible to fill out, using a system of shorthand codes covering every possible situation. As you will see, if you make an entry for each hour, you will have a very complete description of your baby's state of being. Not only will this give you an initial assessment of the situation with regard to your child's crying, but it will allow you to track the infant's behavior as you proceed with the program. Nothing will reassure you more than seeing the total number of minutes of crying diminish day by day.

Another aspect of the behavior diary relates to your behavior, not your baby's. The filled-out diary page will keep track of every one of your responses to the baby's cries as well as the baby's behavior, allowing you to progress from option to option without repeating your-self or becoming confused or forgetful.

Instructions for Filling Out the Diary

You will find a sample Daily Diary Page on page 104. Note that each page is designed for twelve hours, with each line devoted to one hour. Keep this book in a central location out in the open so you remember to make your entries at the end of each hour. (If you would prefer not to write in the book, photocopy the blank forms and keep them on a clipboard in that same central location.) Keep a pen or pencil with the forms to make the filling in of the blanks as easy as possible. And remember, you're not committing yourself to a lifetime of record keeping; you'll just be doing this for a few days. The payoff will be worth the effort.

Prepare yourself mentally to fill out the forms for at least four days, and make your notations as close to each hour as is convenient. This means filling out the day-time columns as they occur; make your notations at the end of every hour. For nighttime hours, remember to describe your baby's sleeping and waking time accurately when you awaken in the morning.

At the end of each twelve-hour shift—that is, when you come to the bottom of each page—take an extra several moments to total the amount of crying time in minutes. Be aware that if you discover that you have missed an hour and can't remember the missing experience, the day's record keeping hasn't been a total loss. But because you'll be working with the program for only a few days, the loss of even an hour's accounting will make a difference in your comparative totals. So make an effort

Daily Diary Page

Name _____ JANE _____

Day/Date _____ January 6 _____

a.m. (p.m.)   (circle one)

Activity Code

S   =   Sleeping alone (not held)
SH =   Sleeping held
F   =   Feeding
AAH =   Awake, alone, and happy (in crib, infant
              seat, swing, etc., but not held)
AAC =   Awake, alone, and crying
AHH =   Awake, held, and happy
AHC =   Awake, held, and crying
(W) =   Being walked
(R) =   Being rocked
B   =   Being bathed
(P) =   Pacifier

Hour	Start Time	Activity	Minutes of Crying
12	Continued	F/12:30 AHH/12:45 AAC (crib)/ 12:50 S	5
1		S	
2		S	
3		S/3:30 F	
4		AHC/4:20 AAH (P) (swing)/ 4:25 AAC/4:30 AHC(W)	45
5		S	15
6		S	
7		B/7:15 F/7:45 AAH (P) (swing)	
8		AAC (swing)/8:10 AHH/ 8:25 AAH (crib)	5
9		S	
10		AAC (crib)/10:20 AHC/ 10:25 SH/10:35 S	10
11		S	

Total minutes crying: 80

to fill in the blanks for every hour religiously, so your records will be accurate.

Use the code to record your baby's behavior. The code is an efficient shorthand that encompasses, in a broad way, each of the possible sleeping and waking states your baby could be in at any one time. Though the codes are simple and self-evident, I'll go through them here one by one to help you become acquainted with the notation system. Eventually, you will memorize them.

•S = *sleeping alone (not held)*. Your baby is asleep anywhere—in the crib, on your bed, in the baby seat, in the car seat. The place makes no difference except that the baby is alone, not in someone's arms.

•SH = *sleeping held*. Your baby is asleep in your arms or the arms of someone else.

•F = *feeding*. Your baby is feeding—either nursing or bottle-feeding. It makes no difference who is feeding the baby.

•AAH = *Awake, alone, and happy*. The infant is wide awake and not being held—for example, in the crib, infant seat, swing, car seat—and not crying. The baby may be vocalizing, perhaps even "threatening" to cry, but he or she is not actually crying.

•AAC = *Awake, alone, and crying*. The infant is awake, not being held, and actively signaling through crying that he or she is in need of a response from you.

•AHH = *Awake, held, and happy*. The baby is being held, by you or someone else, and is not crying. Again, the child may be vocalizing but is not actually crying.

•AHC = *Awake, held, and crying*. The baby is being held, by you or someone else, and is crying. Note: If the baby is being rocked or walked, indicate these variables with an R or a W in parentheses—for example, AHH(W) or AHC(R).

•*B = Bathing.* The child is being bathed, either in a tub or with a sponge.

•*P = Pacifier.* Whenever the baby is sucking the pacifier or the pacifier is being offered but refused, please indicate this in parentheses after the appropriate companion code—for example AAH(P).

On your diary forms, each of these codes will be *preceded* by a number indicating the time the behavior began and *followed* by a slash to show that the behavior has ended. The time noted down for the next behavior, after the slash, will also be the end time for the first behavior.

Whenever the baby is alone—that is, not being held—note down the place, such as crib, infant seat, car seat, and so on.

If a behavior does not begin with 12 but is a continuation from the previous page, note this by writing "continue" in the start time box. For example:

12 noon: At noon Jane was feeding, so "continue" was written in the start time box. Jane remained held and was observed to be happy. At 12:45, Jane was put in her crib and began to cry, and by 12:50 she had fallen asleep. Total minutes of crying: 5.

1:00: Jane was still sleeping and slept through the hour. Total minutes of crying: 0.

2:00: Jane was still sleeping and slept through the hour. Total minutes of crying: 0.

3:00: Jane was still sleeping and slept until 3:30, when she began feeding. Total minutes of crying: 0.

4:00: Feeding proceeded until 4:10, at which time Jane stopped feeding and, still in the arms of the person who fed her, began to cry. She cried until 4:20, when she was given the pacifier and set in her swing. She resumed crying at 4:25. At 4:30, she was picked up and walked. Still crying, she was put down in her crib at 4:35. She continued crying in her crib throughout the hour. Total minutes of crying: 45.

5:00: Jane continued to cry until 5:15, when she fell asleep. Total minutes of crying: 15.

6:00: Jane continued to sleep. Total minutes of crying: 0.

7:00: Jane awoke and was bathed at 7:00, and beginning at 7:15 she was fed. At 7:45, she was given her pacifier to suck on and placed in her swing, where she was observed to be happy. Total minutes of crying: 0.

8:00: Jane remained contentedly sucking on her pacifier in her swing until 8:05, when she began to cry. She was picked up and held at 8:10, at which time she ceased crying, and at 8:25 Jane was put to bed in her crib. She lay awake happily for five minutes, and had drifted off to sleep by 8:30. Total minutes of crying: 5.

9:00: Jane continued to sleep. Total minutes of crying: 0.

10:00: Jane remained asleep until 10:15, when she awoke crying. Her parents were apparently waiting to see whether she would fall back asleep, and picked her up at 10:20. She continued to cry for five minutes, and by 10:25, she had fallen asleep in the arms of her caregiver. At 10:35, still sleeping, Jane was laid in her crib. Total minutes of crying: 10.

11:00: Jane remained asleep for the hour. Total minutes of crying: 0.

Upon finishing the journal page, the notekeeper added up the minutes of crying time for this twelve-hour period: 80.

The next journal page, beginning with 12 midnight, would start with S, to indicate that Jane was still sleeping.

Be as accurate as you can. Every time something changes, record the change with the time the new behavior started. For example, if your baby falls asleep in your arms at 12:50 and is held for ten minutes and then put down, on the line for that hour you would write:

AHH/12:50/1:00 S...

Or say your baby sleeps until 10:15, when he or she begins to cry, but you pick the baby up immediately and he or she instantly stops crying. In this instance you would note:

S/10:15 AAC/10:15 AHH/ ...

But if the baby cried for five minutes in the crib before you picked him or her up, at which time the crying stopped immediately, you would write:

S/10:15 AAC/10:20 AHH/ ...

If the baby woke in the crib and began crying at 9:00, was immediately picked up and rocked, but continued to cry for ten minutes, was walked around the house but continued to cry until finally falling off to sleep after fifteen minutes, at which time you laid the sleeping baby in the crib, you would write:

S/9:00 AAC(C)/9:00 AHC(R)/9:10
AHC(W)/9:25 SH/9:25 S(C)

The Purposes of the Diary

Now you can see why I depend so heavily on the diary pages in my practice to assess the situation when parents bring in a colicky baby. I'm not present in the household when the baby cries; I have to depend solely on the parents' estimate when asking how long the baby has been crying each day. I've found that parents usually overestimate because of their anxiety and exhaustion, but also because they are giving broad estimates in terms of hours, whereas the truly accurate breakdown is given in minutes. The diary code allows you to report changes on a minute-by-minute basis and to add up the total number of minutes, not a general figure rounded off to the nearest hour or half hour.

The first function of the diary, then, is to tell you *precisely* how much your child is crying and to see how that amount compares to the norm of thirty to ninety minutes per twenty-four hours.

The second function of the diary is to track changes in the crying over the course of the program.

And the third function, the most complex, is to show in black and white just what is going on when the baby cries. In short, it allows you to see which responses are effective at any given moment and which ones are not.

PART C: ANALYZING YOUR DIARY

Part C is the phase in which you assess your diary. In Part B you recorded your child's behavior and your responses to that behavior for a twenty-four-hour period and now you will study the two forms you've filled out. Look carefully at the times when your infant cried for long periods and you were unable to console him or her. Are there any times when you waited a long period of time before responding to your baby? Did you continually respond in the same manner without trying a different option? Did you give up trying different options? Did you conclude that the problem was a physical one that you couldn't control—gas, for example? If this is the case, your diary will probably reveal that you tried to comfort your baby by walking or rocking him or her for hours on end, rather than concentrating on meeting the real needs signaled by the cry. Review Chapter 4 and try to determine the reason you were unable to stop your infant's crying. If the crying episode seems to occur around feeding times, concentrate on the section about the need for food; if they occur during attempts to put the baby to sleep, review the section on the need to sleep; and so forth.

PART D: PLANNING A NEW APPROACH

After analyzing your diary, plan a different response to your infant's cries in the future using the principles of this book. I am going to give you two aids to help you do this. The first is three flowcharts designed to help you organize your response to your baby's crying in the different contexts in which they can occur. The second is to give you a program for responding successfully to each specific crying episode within seven minutes. After you have read through this chapter and practiced using the flowcharts and applying the program to your baby, record his or her behavior in the diary for another twenty-four hours. Calculate the amount of crying your infant is doing now. If it's less than ninety minutes—congratulations! We have a cure. If not, don't dismay; it may take several days to achieve success. If the crying is still excessive, analyze this diary as you did the previous one, find your mistakes, and do a third diary. Continue this process until the infant is crying less than ninety minutes. It rarely takes more than five days.

INTERPRETING THE FLOWCHARTS

Flowcharts I, II, and III are designed to help you organize your responses to your baby's crying; they cover all possible messages your baby might be trying to communicate to you, within various contexts. Remember, you need to move through the various options quickly and with a minimum of confusion. If one response doesn't work, move on to the next. I suggest you familiarize yourself with the flowcharts and situations before you actually need to refer to them.

SITUATION #1: CRYING BEGINS DURING FEEDING (FLOWCHART I)

If your baby starts crying while being fed, he or she might be sending you one of several messages. First, the baby could be signaling that he or she is no longer hungry. If you are breast-feeding, a second possibility may be that the baby is still hungry but the breast milk has stopped flowing—that the baby is actually sucking at an empty breast. Another alternative is that the baby is experiencing the fleeting cramping pain associated with the gastrocolic reflex, the normal phenomenon described earlier.

As you can see, the first step is to stop feeding and try to calm the baby. If the crying stops, try to resume feeding.

It is at this point that many parents make the common mistake of assuming the problem is gas. Rather than attempting to resume the feeding, they try to burp

FLOWCHART I

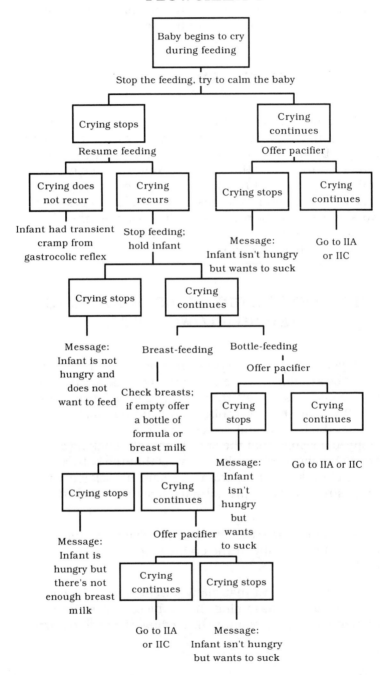

the baby. Since the problem is rarely if ever gas, parents taking this approach inevitably find themselves with a baby crying her way into a highly agitated state.

If, when you attempt to resume feeding, the baby takes the breast or bottle and happily continues to suck, you can assume that the initial cry signaled the transient cramping.

If the baby cries when you attempt to resume feeding but calms down easily when, after a moment, you stop, you can assume that the message inherent in the crying was that the baby is no longer hungry.

If the crying ends when the feeding is stopped (the baby usually stops and waits expectantly once taken from the breast), but then begins very quickly again after feeding is resumed, the baby may be indicating that the flow of milk from the breast has stopped. This message is actually expressed quite characteristically unless the frustration level is very high—the baby eagerly takes the breast, sucks two or three times, and then begins to howl.

When this is the case, check your breast to see whether milk is present. If your breast is full and leaking, the breast milk is obviously present and there is some other explanation for the crying, and you should move on to Flowchart II, A or C. However, if your breast feels empty and it is difficult to express milk from it, the baby may be crying because he or she is still hungry. Offer the second breast. If the crying still continues, then offer the baby a bottle of formula or pumped breast milk.

This option means, of course, that *while you are going through the program, it is necessary to keep a bottle of formula or expressed breast milk on hand for all feedings until you are sure that the milk supply is sufficient.* This bottle should be prepared and ready to use so that, should the necessity to use it arise, not much time elapses.

If the baby who cries when breast-feeding resumes takes the bottle readily without crying, you can assume that he or she was signaling to you that the flow of breast milk was insufficient.

If the baby begins to cry during feeding and takes neither bottle nor breast, offer the pacifier. The baby may not be hungry but might still want to suck. For both breast-fed and bottle-fed babies who continue to cry, refer to A or C of Flowchart II.

NOTE: When there are frequent episodes of crying that begin during feeding and are difficult to resolve using the chart, check to make sure there is no vomiting or diarrhea. If either of these symptoms is present, the problem is not infant colic syndrome but could be a milk allergy or severe cramping related to the gastrocolic reflex. The latter can occur in babies with a narrow anal canal, a condition that can be diagnosed and treated by your physician. *Consult your baby's doctor whenever vomiting or diarrhea occurs.*

SITUATION #2: CRYING BEGINS WHILE THE BABY IS BEING HELD (FLOWCHART II)

If your baby begins to cry while he or she is awake and being held, use your powers of observation and intuition, your knowledge of your baby, and a quick survey of the baby's day in making a judgment as to which trail in Flowchart II to follow first:

- A: Infant appears tired
- B: Infant could be hungry
- C: Infant is awake and probably not hungry

Let's begin with IIA—you believe the baby to be tired. The first step is to place the baby in the crib to see if he or she falls asleep. If the crying stops and the baby falls asleep, your interpretation of the crying was correct.

If the crying continues, don't rush to pick the baby up; your first interpretation might still be correct. Stop

115

FLOWCHART II

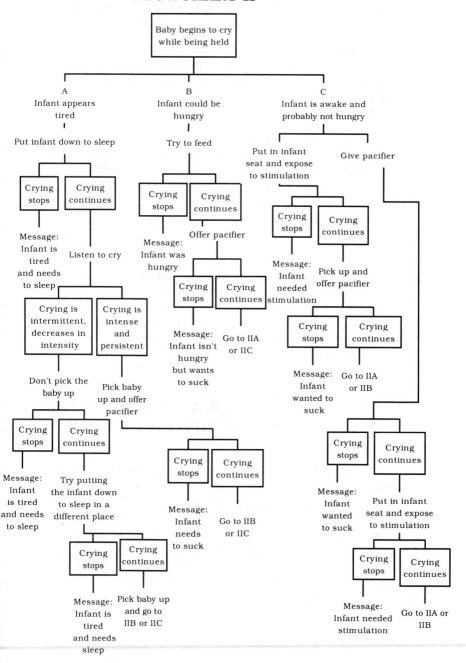

and listen to the crying. If it is becoming intermittent and decreasing in intensity, leave the infant alone; some infants cry in this manner as they fall off to sleep.

If the crying continues in this intermittent manner and doesn't end, move the infant to another place where sleep might come easier. Some babies like sleeping in small enclosed areas such as cradles, while others like to sleep in larger areas such as cribs.

If the cries continue after you put the baby down and have waited for not more than five minutes, assume that he or she is not tired and go to IIB if you think the baby might be hungry. If, while trying to feed the infant as instructed in IIB, the feeding does not stop the crying, try a pacifier. The baby may not be hungry but may want to suck.

If you are assuming that the baby is not hungry, you should try either sitting him or her up to receive stimulation—perhaps in an infant seat in a busy room—or offer a pacifier. Either response would be acceptable at this juncture. If you choose to try stimulation first and it is not successful, offer a pacifier. If you try a pacifier first without success, try stimulation.

SITUATION #3: CRYING BEGINS WHILE THE BABY IS ALONE (FLOWCHART III)

If the baby has been sleeping alone in the crib, infant seat, or swing when the crying occurs, start with A. Remember that babies can cry in their sleep, as part of dream behavior. Since such crying is not communication, it is important to make sure the baby is definitely awake before you pick him or her up. This is particularly relevant if the baby has been asleep for only a short period, one that you expected would last longer.

FLOWCHART III

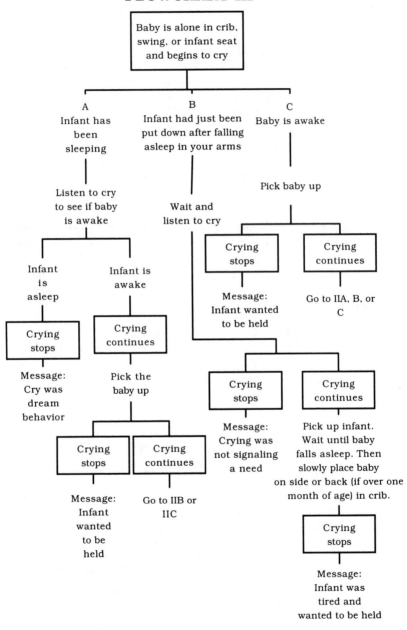

If the baby is awake, pick him or her up. If the crying stops, the message was that the baby wanted to be held, and you indeed responded correctly.

If your infant falls asleep in your arms and awakens crying almost immediately after being put down, follow B. Again, make sure the baby is truly awake before you do anything. If after a minute or two the baby is still crying, pick the baby up and allow him or her to fall asleep again in your arms. At times, infants need to feel physically close to an adult and will awaken as soon as they realize they are no longer being held. The goal is then to get the baby back in the crib or other sleeping place without his or her being aware of the change. For a child older than one month of age, once he or she is in a deep sleep, very slowly move the baby into a horizontal position in your arms. Then gradually—and very care-fully—place the baby in the crib. If the infant is less than a month old, use a rolled-up towel or receiving blanket to prop the baby on his or her side, to prevent aspiration in case the child spits up or vomits.

If your infant has been awake and happy in an in-fant seat, swing, or crib and then begins to cry, follow C by picking the baby up. If the crying stops, the baby was communicating the desire to be picked up. If the crying continues, go back to Flowchart II, B or C.

SITUATION #4: CRYING BEGINS DURING BATHING

Some infants dislike being naked and cry whenever they are undressed. They find the sensation of cool air against their skin unpleasant. Such babies will cry for the entire length of the bathing period, and this crying is very difficult to allay. One suggestion is to bathe the baby in a very warm room—perhaps a bathroom that has been steamed up by the running of a hot shower.

ever leave the baby to cry for more than several
inutes.

e prepared to feed your baby on demand, not on a
redetermined schedule.

old the baby readily whenever necessary.

ffer a pacifier readily.

ealize that simply holding the baby is enough;
ocking and walking the baby are unnecessary dis-
actions.

ERPRETING YOUR BABY'S CRIES BY QUICK TRIAL AND ERROR— IN SEVEN MINUTES

w you are ready to begin to match your responses
urately as possible to your baby's cries by pro-
g in an orderly way to determine precisely which
he infant is signaling at any one time in seven
minutes. The actions you will take are really quite
. The most demanding part of the program will be
ifting of your perspective, which is necessary in
or your responses to be based on messages you've
reted from the cries—not just seen as distressing
ons that must be eliminated.

hieving this perspective shift is really an exercise
centration, requiring that you think deeply about
you are doing and about what is going on with
aby. You are going to have to respond to your baby's
vith a series of actions that you automatically per-
n a quick, orderly movement—a form of guess-
hat covers all possible bases.

te those words *quick* and *orderly*. First, consider
ne element. As you proceed from option to option,
nber that the main objective is to find the right

Of course, it is extremely important to make sure the bath water is not too hot or the baby will be scalded.

SITUATION #5: CRYING BEGINS DURING A CAR RIDE

Safety First! No matter how lustily the baby cries, never take him or her out of the car seat while the car is moving. If you cannot console the baby while the car is in motion, stop the car. Most babies find car rides hypnotic and fall asleep when the car is moving. However, a minority of infants cry whenever they ride in the car. These babies probably have a form of motion sickness, but of course, medication for infants under six months of age is not recommended.

WHAT TO DO IF YOUR BABY BECOMES AGITATED

What should you do if you simply cannot allay your baby's cries and the baby enters that state of agitation in which nothing seems to help? I'm afraid there is no easy solution at this point. You can try alternating between walking the baby and putting him or her in the crib for ten to fifteen minutes at a time, with the hope that sleep will end the cries. If your infant finds car rides hypnotic and you can trust *yourself* to stay awake, try taking the baby for a ride. Your only consolation at this point is to remind yourself that with the advice of this book and the program to guide you, such episodes of agitation should be truly unusual.

THE PROGRAM

The problem you face is to determine why exactly your baby is crying and what the accurate response is to the specific message in the cry. This is no easy task when you are dealing with an infant who cannot talk and, in the case of a colicky baby, is by temperament not one to give up easily. To interpret the different signals accurately, it is important that you approach the crying in an organized way.

For this approach to work, however, you must be guided by the assumption that your crying baby is attempting to communicate a specific message to you—is, in fact, asking you for something. Your goal each time the baby cries is to respond with precisely what the baby needs.

Answering with the Right Response

Remember, when you begin, that there are only five different things a healthy baby can signal for with his or her cries—only five possible needs that must be met. To reiterate, these needs are:

1. The need for food
2. The need for sleep
3. The need to suck
4. The need to be held
5. The need for stimulation

And for every one of these needs, there is only a very limited number of correct responses:

1. *For the need for food:* feeding on demand, regardless of when the last feeding took place.

2. *For the need for sle*
determining how the baby [
(in the parents' arms, in a c
such as a bassinet, or in a l
movement) and then puttin

3. *For the need to suck:*
can be a restricting and th
tion for some mothers) or,
former, a pacifier.

4. *For the need to be hel*
ing the baby. There is no ne
need of holding, and there
concerned about "spoiling"
her too much.

5. *For the need for stim*
an infant seat in a room whe
placing the baby in an infan
to him or her. For most babi
such stimulation is usually e

This handful of options i
They are all you need to offe
quire. Any cry in a healthy ba
these few responses—as long
quickly enough. If the delay be
munication and the correct re
may grow so agitated by frus
be unable to respond to your
explained, in babies who are l
in their demands, it is this de
tation that together cause wh
drome. One more point needs
its importance. To respond di
munications, you must be p
needs. If you retain certain pr
able to offer the accurate res
baby will cry himself into an
open yourself to these points:

answer before the baby grows frustrated and too agitated to respond even when the right need is met. With this approach you will be able to respond to your infant's cry within a short seven minutes.

It is not too far from the truth to describe the process as a game, a form of charades, in which you must guess the meaning of a message acted out by a player who doesn't possess verbal communication skills. You must come up with the right answer before the time runs out. Though this time period varies from child to child, it usually takes a good fifteen minutes before a baby is so agitated that nothing will work.

As to proceeding in an *orderly* manner, the flowcharts on pages 112, 115, and 117 will help you with that. Follow the options presented in the charts (and explained on pages 111-118), moving from one to another within minutes. Try not to repeat yourself, use common sense (for example, attempt to feed the baby before trying anything else if the child has not eaten recently), but don't allow yourself to be ruled by logic (even if feeding has occurred recently, do try to feed the baby if nothing else has worked).

For an example of both a shift in perspective and a fast, orderly approach to interpretation, let's look at two scenarios drawn from an earlier hypothetical example—Billy's story. In the first scenario, the parents are governed by their anxiety for their child along with an over-riding desire to put an end to the crying—without discerning the message it carries. In the second scenario, the parents respond from the perspective that crying is communication and use this program to quell the crying in less than seven minutes.

The Wrong Way. Lois and Tom hear their two-month-old son, Billy, cry. It is ten at night. They look at the clock and notice that the infant has slept for only one hour. Feeling that Billy needs more sleep, they let him cry for another ten minutes, hoping he will fall asleep. However, Billy is hungry, and rather than fall asleep, he continues to cry nonstop as loudly as he can. Finally, Tom and Lois go into Billy's room—the baby is sweaty and red in the face and as he cries, he draws up his legs and hardens his abdomen. Several times he passes gas, so the parents conclude that their baby is experiencing gas pains. Lois picks Billy up and walks with him while patting him on the back. Not only is the infant hungry now, but he is also quite angry. He continues to cry for an additional ten minutes while Lois and Tom trade off holding and walking with him. Unsure about what is going on and growing very anxious, the parents put the infant in a swing and try singing to him. Billy—hungry, angry, and frustrated—continues to wail.

Finally, after Billy has cried for thirty minutes straight, Lois tries to breast-feed him. However, by this time, Billy is too agitated to stop crying immediately and feed. Lois doesn't realize this, and only sees that the infant is refusing the breast. Giving up, she begins to walk him around the house again. During this time, the infant does stop crying, but he starts up again as soon as the walking stops. After an hour of this, Tom and Lois put Billy in his crib. After crying for ten more minutes, the exhausted baby drops off to sleep.

The Right Way. If Lois and Tom were using my program, this is how they would have responded to the following crying episode. They hear their baby crying. It is ten at night. They look at the clock and see that the baby has slept for only one hour. Since they hope Billy is crying in his sleep and is not really ready to get up, they follow the flowchart beginning at IIIA. Billy's cry is intense, continuous, and loud. Tom picks Billy up, sits down in a chair and cuddles him. But after a minute, Billy is still crying and Tom, believing it unlikely that Billy is hungry, having fed him just before his bedtime, starts to follow the responses in Flowchart IIC. He decides to first offer him a pacifier. Billy takes and sucks on it for about thirty seconds, then he lets it drop and begins to cry again even more loudly than before.

Now Lois puts the baby in an infant seat and tries talking to him. This also fails to stop the crying and after two minutes, Lois, moving on to the IIB track, puts Billy to her breast. The baby stops crying and breast-feeds for fifteen minutes, after which he falls back to sleep.

Analysis. In the first scenario, Tom and Lois initially ignored their baby's crying. When the crying failed to abate, they assumed from the look of the child that he was in pain. Somewhat later, they simply gave up on determining why Billy was crying and gave no further thought to why the child was crying. They didn't consider the possibility that the cries carried a message regarding a specific need. As a result, it took them an hour and forty minutes to stop the infant's crying.

In the second scenario, the parents assumed that the cries were cries of communication and used the program to discover the cause of the crying in only five and a half minutes. That was all it took them to successfully hit on the correct response, putting an end to Billy's crying.

SAY GOOD-BYE TO COLIC

As I have said throughout this book, babies vary, making predictions as to their precise responses impossible. Still, if you use the program by following the different paths of options on the flowcharts, remain calm, move from option to option in a quick and orderly fashion—you will be able to meet your baby's needs and stop the crying in seven minutes or less. If your baby has infant colic syndrome, his or her crying time will fall to well within the normal range (thirty to ninety minutes) within a few days—one week at most.

If, even before you start the program, your baby's crying time falls within the normal range, you will still benefit from using the flowcharts, since they can help you respond to your baby's cries with great accuracy and a minimum of delay or confusion.

Finally, if you are reading this book while you await the arrival of your baby, you will have grounded yourself in a basic principle that until now has received too little attention in both the medical and lay worlds—that the baby's cries carry messages and that to interpret those cries accurately and respond to them appropriately is to foster a sense of security in the child that cannot be nurtured in any other way.

By the time your child is eight months old, that general sense of security will have evolved into a strong attachment with the baby's main care-giver—usually the mother, but quite possibly the father or another person intimately involved in caring for the child. This attachment, which I refer to in this book as infant-parent attachment, is absolutely essential to a child's healthy psychological and social adjustment. When this bond is weak or troubled, problems inevitably follow. By using this program, you are taking the positive steps toward ensuring the strength of this essential link between you and your baby. Researchers have determined that the element most essential to the strength of that bond is the parents' responsiveness to crying. In the next chapter, we will explore the infant-parent bond and its significance in greater detail.

Alex: Crying and the Need to Feed

When I first saw Alex in my office, he was eight weeks old. His parents reported to me that he cried approximately four to five hours every day—every evening from six to ten. His parents were exhausted and didn't think they could take much more.

Alex had been six pounds, ten ounces, at birth. His delivery and time spent in the nursery were normal. He had no vomiting or diarrhea; his bowel movements, which he had once or twice a day, were soft; and he had been gaining weight nicely. My physical examination showed him to be a healthy, normal baby. What was he eating? I asked. The answer was soy-based formula, and yes, his mother told me, they were feeding him on demand.

Mr. and Mrs. Brecher were convinced that Alex was having abdominal pain. Alex's previous pediatrician had agreed and suggested many formula changes—all with no reduction in the crying episodes. So the parents decided to seek a second opinion and came to me.

I had Mr. and Mrs. Brecher keep a seventy-two-hour diary for me. The journal showed that Alex was crying three hours and six minutes a day, considerably less than the parents had reported. This did not surprise me, since in my experience the parents' estimate is usually one to one and a half times greater than the actual number of minutes recorded in the diary. Still, Alex's crying was well outside the normal range of thirty to ninety minutes per twenty-four hours. As the parents had reported, the episodes usually began around six in the evening, about two to two and a half hours after a feeding. At other times of the day, during which there were no extended crying episodes, Alex fed every three and a half to four hours.

The diary showed that Mrs. Brecher responded to Alex's crying episodes either by giving him a pacifier, putting him in his crib, or walking with him. She never offered him a bottle until the crying had gone on for at least forty-five minutes, and then it never seemed to be effective. I asked the parents why they never tried to feed Alex sooner during the course of a crying spell.

"But he's never hungry until three and a half to four hours after a feeding," they told me. It never occurred to them that the baby might be hungry when he began cry-ing at six in the evening. When I suggested that possibil-ity, Mrs. Brecher told me she was worried about feeding Alex too frequently. Yes, they were feeding on demand, she told me, but in fact they were placing some limitations on the frequency of the feedings. "I don't want to overfeed him," Mrs. Brecher said worriedly.

I assured the Brechers that Alex did indeed have in-fant colic syndrome—he met all the criteria—and asked if they would be willing to change their approach. When they assured me they would gladly try anything at this point, I suggested that they offer Alex a bottle immediately when he began crying in the early evening, even though he had been fed two or two and a half hours previously. They did this and the next two diary pages showed a reduction in crying from three hours and six minutes to only an aver-age of an hour and fifteen minutes a day. The record showed that Alex was feeding every four to five hours during the night and every three and a half to four hours in the daytime except during the evening, when he was ready to eat two hours after the previous feeding.

This case history illustrates several points. The first is that parents should always assume that a cry might be one of hunger. It is certainly reasonable to try a pacifier or to try holding the baby before offering him a bottle, but if these maneuvers don't end the crying, a bottle should be the next option regardless of how much time has passed since the previous feeding.

Also, as Alex's story shows, the parents need to move through the options quickly. The Brechers waited too long—a full forty-five minutes into the crying episode—and by that time the baby was far too agitated to take the bottle. In his refusal, he was confirming the Brechers' assump-tion that Alex wasn't hungry, thus making it even less likely that they would respond to the cries as signals of hunger.

Finally, the story nicely illustrates a pattern of crying episodes common in cases of infant colic syndrome. The worst periods of crying occur in the evening. One reason for this is that this period is often the infant's longest stretch of wakefulness and therefore he or she expends more energy than usual. This was precisely the case with Alex—he stayed up longer and got hungrier more quickly. As soon as the Brechers' responses to him became more flexible through using the program, they began truly feeding him on demand and the crying episodes diminished.

Casey: Crying and the Need to Feed

Mr. and Mrs. O'Neal brought in their infant son, Casey, when he was seven weeks old. The couple had another child, Alice, who was three years old. They told me Casey often experienced severe abdominal pain when he fed. They suspected gas, and their pediatrician appeared to agree. He had suggested frequent burpings and some changes in Mrs. O'Neal's breast-feeding techniques, but these had had no effect. Mrs. O'Neal became concerned that she might be eating something that was upsetting her baby's stomach. Her friends and her pediatrician mentioned foods that might produce gas in the baby, and by the time I saw the family, she had eliminated milk, spicy foods, caffeine, and leafy vegetables from her diet. Nothing had helped, however. Mrs. O'Neal told me that during at least one and usually two feedings a day, Casey got violent stomach cramps. These occurred almost immediately after he began to nurse—he would draw up his legs, harden his abdomen, and cry forcefully, the pain seeming to get worse as the feedings progressed.

During these troubled feedings, Mrs. O'Neal was usually able to get Casey to feed only from one breast. The infant appeared to be in too much pain to take the second breast, and his crying would often last up to an hour after the feeding ended.

My examination revealed Casey to be completely normal: his abdomen was soft, his rectal exam was normal, and his weight was right on target. The O'Neals reported that there was no vomiting or diarrhea and they agreed to fill out the diary. It showed that Casey was crying about two hours and 45 minutes every day. About three and a half hours after feeding, Casey would be sitting contentedly in an infant swing, Mrs. O'Neal would pick him up and begin to feed him, and the crying would begin. I went over the diary with the O'Neals and asked Mrs. O'Neal what signal Casey was giving that caused her to think he was hungry and wanted to feed. "Nothing specific," she answered. "I just knew it was time. I fed Alice the same way—never waited until she cried but knew she'd be ready every three and a half hours. It always worked like a charm. Alice hardly ever cried."

I raised the possibility that perhaps Casey wasn't hungry at all when she tried to feed him and perhaps his crying signified that he just wasn't ready. Mrs. O'Neal was skeptical, but the parents agreed not to feed Casey until he fussed or cried. With this change, Casey sometimes went four and a quarter to four and a half hours without fussing or crying to be fed—and the crying episodes during feedings disappeared completely. At the end of several days, Casey's recorded crying time was less than an hour a day.

This story emphasizes an important point about demand feeding. The term means exactly what it says: The baby is fed when he or she demands to be fed. Trying to feed an infant who is not hungry can cause as much crying as trying not to feed a hungry infant.

Also note that these parents came to me because they believed their infant to be in pain. Why? Because he appeared to be in pain. The way he cried, the expression on his face, and his body language all suggested to them that this baby was having painful abdominal cramps. But the fact is, all crying babies look this way. One must do a little more detective work before concluding that pain is causing the crying.

The story dramatizes two other points that need emphasis when infant colic syndrome is at issue. Well-meant but inaccurate advice—both from friends and physician—contributed to the O'Neals' difficulty in interpreting Casey's messages. All these outside sources agreed that Casey's problem was probably pain caused by gas, and the net effect was a complex set of steps involving burping the baby, altering nursing techniques, and changing the mother's diet. As it turned out, this complex approach only made things worse by obscuring the real message in Casey's cries: "I'm not hungry. Don't feed me."

Parental expectations also confused the situation. Given Alice's responses, Mrs. O'Neal expected Casey to be happy when she offered the breast every three and a half hours. Her previous experience hadn't prepared her for a baby with very different preferences. Some babies who are offered the breast without being hungry would have fussed initially and then fed quietly. Others would not have protested at all. But Casey was an expressive baby with a tenacious temperament. He continued to cry for as long as his mother attempted to breast-feed, eventually—and inevitable—becoming inconsolably agitated.

Evan: Crying and the Need for Sleep

Mr. and Mrs. Rinehart came to see me with their five-week-old infant, Evan, because the baby never slept and always seemed tired. The same could be said of the Rineharts—they hardly slept anymore and were always tired. They told me that whenever they tried to put Evan in his crib, he cried. They tried walking him, singing to him, bringing the stroller inside—nothing worked. A friend suggested that they take him for a ride in the car, but this didn't help either. Evan would stop crying for the duration of the car ride but would always begin again the minute the car stopped. The effort of leaving the house and driving around just wasn't worth the temporary silence it brought.

Unlike many parents in this situation, the Rineharts never laid the crying baby down in his crib, believing that it was wrong to let a helpless baby cry for hours on end—to which I agreed.

I examined Evan, found him healthy, and asked the parents to keep the seventy-two-hour diary. The record clearly revealed a pattern. Evan would awaken from his sleep in quite a pleasant mood, and then he would feed well and for the next hour or so remain awake and happy—in his mother's arms, a swing, or an infant seat. He would then become fussy, refuse a pacifier or a bottle, and as soon as he was put down in the crib he would begin to cry. Immediately, one of the Rineharts would pick up the baby and begin to walk with him. Evan would continue to cry and work himself into a state of agitation.

Many infants cry for a few minutes in the process of falling off to sleep. If parents react by picking up the infant, they will actually prevent the child from falling asleep. The entries in the Rineharts' behavior diary on Evan led me to suspect that this was the case here. I asked the Rineharts to place Evan in his crib when he appeared tired and to refrain from picking him up for a few minutes if he began to cry in the crib. "Listen carefully to the cry," I coached them, "to see if it gradually decreases in intensity over ten minutes or so. If the crying is continuous and, rather than diminishing, grows louder and more intense in ten minutes, definitely pick him up and try to quiet him."

The Rineharts practiced this approach scrupulously over the next few days and found that a few minutes after being placed in the crib Evan would fall asleep. Soon the episodes of inconsolable crying were a thing of the past.

Wendy: Crying and the Needs To Suck and Be Held

Mr. and Mrs. Gordon brought in their nine-week-old Wendy, who appeared to want to suck at the breast almost all the time. Whenever she wasn't at the breast, she was crying. Mrs. Gordon felt that she had to come up with a better alternative, but Wendy had refused supplemental bottles or pacifiers. The Gordons' former pediatrician diagnosed Wendy as a colicky baby who would improve over time, and he counseled patience. When Wendy's neediness became too overwhelming, he advised, Mrs. Gordon should put Wendy down and let her cry it out.

The Gordons' behavior diary on Wendy revealed that the baby's episodes of inconsolable crying usually began when Mrs. Gordon took Wendy from the breast and put her in her swing or crib. The baby would begin to cry at this and after twenty to twenty-five minutes of continuous crying, Mrs. Gordon would pick Wendy up and try to console her by putting her back to the breast or walking her. Usually these efforts were unsuccessful. Wendy would go on to cry for as long as an hour until she finally fell asleep.

I asked Mrs. Gordon to try to avoid allowing Wendy to cry continuously for more than five minutes, even if this meant constantly putting her to the breast. She was, for the next several days, to put Wendy to the breast as frequently and as long as necessary to keep her from crying.

Mrs. Gordon followed my advice and Wendy's crying did indeed diminish, but the situation continued to be intolerable for Mrs. Gordon, for Wendy was still at the breast nearly nonstop. Nevertheless, we now knew exactly what Wendy was communicating with her cries: She wanted, in no uncertain terms, to be sucking at her mother's breast. Many of Wendy's needs were fulfilled there. When she was hungry she received calories in the form of breast milk. When she was not hungry but wanted to suck, the breast functioned as a pacifier. And when she wanted to be held and consoled, she felt warm and secure in her mother's arms.

Now that we understood the message, we could set about to improve the situation for Mrs. Gordon. I advised Mrs. Gordon to carry a pacifier with her all the time, continually offering it to Wendy in the hope that the baby would *eventually take it. Also, whenever possible, Mr. Gordon was to hold Wendy and Mrs. Gordon was to leave the room. Once a day, Mr. Gordon offered Wendy pumped breast milk from the bottle.*

Slowly, over time, the situation improved. Wendy eventually began to accept the pacifier during the day. Also, she started taking the supplemental bottle from her father.

Of course, while the parents were working on these adjustments, there were times when Wendy had episodes of inconsolable crying. When they occurred, her parents understood the message but agreed, as I did, that responding accurately was simply not possible. There were times during the day when Mrs. Gordon, owing to her responsibilities to her other children, was simply unable to hold Wendy at her breast. I don't think these episodes were ultimately harmful to Wendy in any way. As long as the parents loved their infant, understood why she was crying, and did their best to prevent it, no damage was done. I stressed this point to Mrs. Gordon, assuring her that she had correctly interpreted Wendy's messages and she had no reason to feel guilty if Wendy's needs conflicted at times with those of her other children. As parents raising children, we are always faced with compromises; for the Gordons, with Wendy the unavoidable compromises began early.

Trevor: Crying and the Need for Stimulation

At ten weeks of age, Trevor seemed to sleep less than most babies, and Mr. and Mrs. Anderson worried about that, as they would have worried about any difference Trevor showed from the norm. They were first-time parents and they wanted to go by the book, but Trevor wasn't cooperating.

They came to me because Trevor cried most of the day. He was a large baby with a big appetite and he soon took to sleeping through the night, from his last feeding at eleven o'clock all the way through to six in the morning. At night, Trevor seemed too good to be true; it was daytime that was the Andersons' nightmare. Trevor would feed eagerly and lie quietly in his mother's arms for up to an hour after his feeding. But when Mrs. Anderson put him down in his crib, he would cry himself into a frenzy of agitation.

I studied the Andersons' diary and questioned them closely—it was obvious that they expected Trevor to sleep substantially after every feeding. After all, didn't all babies nap after they fed? They hated the idea of Trevor's spitting up, and believed napping essential to his digestion. They considered the afternoon nap following the midday feeding particularly important.

I posed the possibility that Trevor was simply not much of a daytime sleeper—unfortunately, perhaps, for parents who could use some time to regroup but possible nevertheless. I suggested that instead of putting the baby down to sleep after the feeding, when Mrs. Anderson needed to get on with other things, that she put him in his infant seat and place him where he could see her as she moved around doing her work. Not until Trevor signaled his need to end the stimulation period by beginning to fuss would they put Trevor in his crib for a nap.

Trevor was indeed a wide-awake baby. His need for sleep during the day was minimal, but he sat quite happily in his seat when there was enough going on around him to remind him he was not alone. The Andersons soon learned, however, that Trevor's period of contentment in a busy room was limited to about half an hour (quite a generous amount of time for a baby of his age), and they needed to be quick to interpret his message when that period came to an end. At that point, Trevor would go off to sleep with a minimum of crying for a short nap, only to awaken a short time later for a feeding.

Chapter 6
The Infant-Parent Relationship in the First Year of Life

"If there were only a key, a secret to all this," parents of infants often say to me in office visits. The essence of what they are saying, I believe, is, "How, really, should I raise my child? How should I treat my infant in the first year of life?" The specific questions and problems that trouble them are legion: Should I feed my infant on a schedule so our lives are regulated and smooth—the way my mother said she raised me—or should I feed him on demand? How can I be sure I won't spoil my baby if I respond each time she cries? Is it possible to hold the baby too much? Should I really guard against being manipulated by my month-old baby, as my father warns I should? Can I teach my nine-month-old not to touch an expensive eighteenth-century Chinese porcelain bowl, or should I put it in a different spot?

Getting to know and adjusting to the presence of a new baby can be a mysterious, demanding, and often frustrating experience. How do we fathom the baby's strange inner world where basic needs clamor and all sensory information a newborn baby receives is new and unorganized? How can we be sure we are laying a sturdy foundation in our interactions with our young children?

I believe, however, that there is a key, one word to describe the ideal parenting approach in the first year of life—responsiveness. If you concentrate your efforts on responding to the messages conveyed in your baby's cries, you will be both keeping your baby physically healthy and laying the groundwork for his or her psychological and cognitive growth. Since the 1970s, science has learned a great deal about child rearing in the first year of life.

MATERNAL-INFANT BONDING

One scientific concept that emerged in 1976 was widely reported and eventually became very well known to the public. It had wide-ranging effects in the medical world and led to important changes in the ways doctors, nurses, and hospitals treated birth and infancy. Ultimately, however, the conclusions of this research were shown to be incorrect.

"Maternal-infant bonding" is a theory described in a book of the same name by Drs. Klaus and Kennell. There these doctors suggest that the first few hours after birth are vital—in fact, the *most* vital—to the relationship of mother and infant. Basing their conclusions on observations of both animals and humans, they argue that in this period, a mother is at her most receptive to both psychological and physical signals sent by her new infant. These signals, facial expressions, and patterns of body language, cause the mother to touch, fondle, and hold the baby, and this reciprocal communication—the baby's signals and the mother's responses—results in what these researchers call the *bonding* of the baby and the mother. This bond, they assert further, is the basis for the baby's future psychological development and relationships with other people.

Clearly, these writers conclude, the mother who begins to hold and nurse her baby immediately after birth will bond with her infant and her infant will bond with her. Conversely, they suggest, in cases where the mother does *not* immediately hold and nurse the baby, the critical bonding will not occur, or it will occur imperfectly. Maternal-infant bonding weakened in this way, the theory goes, means a less than ideal mother-infant relationship.

But what about mothers and infants unavoidably separated at birth, perhaps through the illness of one or the other? Yes, these relationships are at risk, the theorist argues.

There is a positive side to this theory, too, however. In 1976, many people were raising the issue of curbing medicine's high use of technology in the delivery room. The natural childbirth movement was gaining more and more advocates for drug-free childbirth, and the idea that childbirth was a normal expression of health and well-being rather than a medical situation to be treated as an abnormal condition was surfacing. During this time, when the importance of the emotional as well as physical experience of birth was being emphasized for both mother and baby, the maternal-infant bonding theory was received enthusiastically.

The theory's popularity pressured hospitals to stop treating the birth of a baby as a disease and hospitals and medical personnel began to soften their often intrusive, high-tech approach. Birth centers began to appear, in which delivery occurred in a homey atmosphere among practitioners trained to attune themselves to the emotional and psychological environment while still screening the birth process for possible problems.

In these less highly technologized settings, fathers, who before had no place whatsoever in the labor or delivery room, were soon routinely allowed not only to observe but even to participate as labor coaches in the births of their babies. And whereas it was the common practice in the preceding decades to anesthetize women for delivery and to care for the baby in the nursery for as long as twenty-four hours following the birth, mothers were now encouraged to hold and even nurse their babies immediately after birth. Many hospitals instituted "rooming in," whereby the babies could stay in the mothers' hospital rooms rather than in the nursery during their hospital stay.

The notion that the first several hours of interrelating were critical to the mother-infant relationship also influenced those medical professionals who cared for ill newborns. These babies had been routinely isolated from their parents, but now physicians and nurses in infant intensive care units began to allow parents to see and interact with their babies and even, where possible, to become involved in their care.

All of these truly positive changes, which have done much to make parents across the nation feel more comfortable and competent with their babies, can be at least partially ascribed to the influence of Klaus's and Kennell's theory of maternal-infant bonding. And yet under close examination, the theory has not held up over time. Comparisons of the mother-infant relationship among mothers and infants who have been together since birth and mothers and infants who had been separated for several days after birth reveal no significant differences. Some studies showed *short-term* positive effects of being together from birth, but none showed any long-term negative effects of being separated at birth. Now experts agree that there is no critical period during which mothers and infants are particularly sensitive to each other. In fact, scientists now believe that a mother's love can overcome and compensate for any separation that might occur directly after birth. Studies have shown that the relationship between a mother and infant develops not over hours and days, as Klaus's and Kennell's theory had it, but over weeks and months. The fact is that mother-infant attachment develops over the entire first year of the baby's life. Everything else being normal, this attachment develops *despite* separations that might occur in the first few days of life.

The basic developmental task that is accomplished during the first year of a baby's life is the securing of a healthy parent-infant attachment, or relationship, and everything that happens to the baby and parent in the course of that year is a part of the developmental process. Furthermore, the reciprocal communication process that occurs when the baby cries and the parent responds is central to the building of this psychological foundation.

INFANT-PARENT ATTACHMENT

You may already have noticed that scientific study of infants up to very recently has focused exclusively on infants' relationships with their mothers. Although this is somewhat a matter of convention, in most cultures, even highly developed ones, mothers are still most often the primary care-givers for children. Most literature refers exclusively to the mother-infant attachment, since that is the specific relationship that has fallen under scrutiny. I, however, do not necessarily make the assumption that the mother is the baby's exclusive care-giver, or that the strongest parental bond is with the mother. I believe that the main relationship is with the *primary* care-giver. Therefore, I prefer to use the term *infant-parent attachment.*

Infant Attachment Behaviors

It was John Bowlby who developed the theory of infant-maternal attachment, asserting that the relationship between baby and mother during the first year of life was the foundation of human development. As evidence, he pointed out that in a culture of hunters and gatherers, the infant who remains close to an adult has the best chance for survival. Since those babies who survive to adulthood perpetuate the species and thus their genetic characteristics, Bowlby felt it safe to assume that infant behavior that brought an adult close—called *attachment behavior*—was favored by evolution.

What are the "attachment behaviors" that form the infant's side of the infant-mother relationship? Those evidenced in the first few months of life are crying, smiling, clinging, and sucking. As the child develops more motor skills, crawling and grasping become important, and as the child's language skills progress, the baby learns to use babbling and other forms of vocalizing to bring the mother close.

The smile, too, is a form of attachment behavior—an ingenious one, as Bowlby describes it. The first infant's smiles, which occur in the second month, are spontaneous, but soon the baby begins to smile in response to the sight of a face. But that's only half of the story. Bowlby suggests that the smile triggers an instinctive, genetically programmed set of behaviors in the mother—fondling, holding, and talking. In this sense, we might view the smile as a delightful expression of the connectedness between mother and infant. How satisfying it is actually to see evidence of the link!

Crying—our subject of concern in this book—is also an important central attachment behavior in the human infant. In fact, crying is probably the infant's most effective means of bringing the mother close during the first three months of life. If you still have qualms about the potential of "spoiling" your infant by responding to his or her cries, it should help you to understand that those cries are built-in mechanisms for ensuring that the baby is looked after.

In studying these attachment behaviors, Bowlby concludes that in addition to serving an evolutionary purpose—that of keeping the species alive and thriving—they also served a psychological function. Added together, the infant's attachment signals and the mother's responses result in the first relationship the infant experiences. It is this relationship that Bowlby calls the infant-mother attachment...and it is the communication at the basis of this relationship that has been the subject of this book.

THE DEVELOPMENT OF THE RELATIONSHIP

An understanding of how this first relationship develops should help you in your effort to interpret your baby's cries. There are four phases of the development of the infant-mother relationship, each phase relating to the level of the infant's cognitive (thinking) and motor (moving) ability.

Phase 1 is particularly relevant here, because it covers the period in which colic is most prevalent—the first three months after birth. During this period, a baby's vision is too weak to enable him or her to discriminate among people; nor does he or she have enough experience to distinguish particular sounds or odors. When the baby feels a need, such as hunger, he or she instinctively performs an attachment behavior—perhaps first by staring, then smiling and fussing, and finally crying. With increasing intensity, these instinctive actions trigger instinctive responses in the mother—to approach and then feed the baby.

Even though it was mothers who were studied and observed, in this phase the baby is not signaling any specific individual—even any individual at all. Rather, the baby is simply driven by instinct to cry into the unknown, with no understanding that there are people out there who can respond. Still, as the parents receive and respond to the baby's signals, the baby gradually becomes aware of and secure in the knowledge that the environment *is* responsive. One might say that the parents' responses actually teach the infant that someone is there to react to his or her cries. In this context, it is clear that your responsiveness as a parent means a great deal more than simply meeting the baby's physical needs.

In Phase 2 of the relationship, which spans the fourth through the sixth month, babies are aware that their mothers (or primary care-givers) are responding to most of their communications. They now have the ability to discriminate among different people, and they respond to their mothers differently from the way they respond to others—smiling in a special way when they see them or crying in a special way when they leave, and reacting in a distinctive way to their mother's face and voice.

In Phase 3, months seven through eight, most babies have some degree of locomotion and can maintain closeness with their mothers not merely by signaling but by voluntarily moving after them. During this phase, the baby exhibits "stranger anxiety," crying at the approach of a stranger or when the mother leaves.

By Phase 4, which begins at nine months of age, a reciprocal relationship between mother and infant is fully developed—each responding to the other's signals. Fully functioning, it now serves as the foundation for the infant's continued psychological and cognitive development.

The process I have described is the normal course of development of the maternal-infant attachment, but what happens when something goes wrong—for instance, when the infant's signals are not met? In an English orphanage study, infants were cared for on a specific schedule but their attachment behaviors were completely ignored. Their smiles or cries evoked no closeness, no reaction of any kind. As a consequence, these babies failed to develop any attachment whatsoever to another human being. And as a result of that, they lost interest in eating, grew poorly, and exhibited extremely retarded social behavior. By any standards, the failure of the care-givers to respond was absolutely catastrophic for these babies' physical, psychological, cognitive, and social development.

SCRUTINIZING THE RELATIONSHIP

In this way, we came to understand the normal relationship as Bowlby described it and, sadly, we know what happens when no such relationship exists at all. But what about the gradations in between? How is the mother-child relationship affected by different levels of parental responsiveness? Armed with John Bowlby's theories, researcher Mary D. Salter Ainsworth and her associates set out to determine in detail what this primary human relationship between infant and mother consisted of and how such relationships compared when levels of parental responsiveness differed.

Ainsworth's first task was to evaluate the strength of the infant-mother attachment among different infant-mother pairs. (No similar study involving fathers has been conducted so far.) She devised a situation that was mildly stressful to the infant—what she called a "stranger situation":

1. A stranger (the examiner) brings mother and child into a room and then leaves.

2. The mother sits passively, allowing the baby to do as he or she wishes; then she encourages the baby to play with the available toys.

3. The stranger returns and relates to the baby.

4. The mother leaves the room.

5. The stranger leaves and the mother returns.

6. The mother tries to involve the baby with the toys once again.

7. The mother leaves.

8. The stranger enters again and tries to relate to the baby.

9. The stranger leaves and the mother returns.

At each of these stages, the baby's reaction is observed closely through a two-way mirror and these questions are addressed:

- Does the baby explore the room freely or cling to the mother?

- Is the baby sociable with or frightened by the stranger?

- With the stranger alone, does the baby play, show fear, or show concern that the mother has left?

- When the mother returns, does the baby rush to be with her, ignore her, or cry?

- How does the baby respond during the second cycle, beginning with step 8?

By answering these and similar questions, the examiners were able to classify the infant-mother relationships they observed into three main groups. The first group consisted of infants whose attachment to the mother was secure. These children, when they were with the stranger, showed an active, clear-cut desire to be reunited with their mothers, actively sought the mothers out when they returned, exhibited attachment behavior, and responded positively when their mothers picked them up and held them. When these babies were alone in the room with their mothers, they were secure enough to wander away and explore their new environments.

In the second group, the infant-mother attachment was highly abnormal. The babies showed no signs of stress when the mothers left the room and either ignored or avoided the mothers when they returned. In the final group, the attachment was abnormal as well, but not as critically so as in the second group. Infants in this group seemed to want or miss their mothers but when reunited showed signs of ambivalence and even resistance. Also, when these babies were alone with their mothers in the room, unlike the securely attached infants, they did not leave their mothers to explore the new environment but rather clung to them, never leaving their sides.

From Ainsworth's observations, we can summarize two conditions—secure and insecure infant attachment—in this way:

Infants with a Secure Infant-Mother Attachment

1. Use the mother as a secure base for exploration

2. Show stress when the mother leaves the room

3. Actively seek to join the mother when she returns

4. At home (gathered in the second phase of the research, which I will soon describe) are always aware of the mother's whereabouts and follow her from room to room

5. Generally do not become overdistressed when the mother leaves and cannot be followed

Infants with an Insecure Infant-Mother Attachment

1. Either constantly cling to the mother or ignore her completely

2. When the mother leaves become either frantic and angry or apathetic

3. At reunion, show ambivalence and anger or ignore or avoid the mother

4. At home either cling to the mother constantly, showing extreme stress when she leaves, or seem unable to relate to her and demonstrate affection, showing no evidence of attachment to her at all

Now Ainsworth had a detailed description of normal and abnormal infant-mother attachments for infants of one year of age. Her next step was to send observers into family homes to discover which behavior on the mother's part led to the secure attachment and which resulted in an insecure attachment. Following the observations, which went on over the course of a year, the mothers' behavior was analyzed and correlated with the strength of the relationship.

The following are the results:

Mothers of Infants Exhibiting Secure Infant-Mother Attachments

1. Were highly sensitive to their babies, making themselves psychologically accessible in a way that the other group did not

2. Attempted to view the world from their babies' point of view in order to "tune in" to the infants' needs—a clear reference to their attempts to understand the babies' messages

3. Noticed their babies' signals and responded promptly

4. When their babies' behavior was annoying or irritating, accepted it without anger or resentment

5. Treated their babies as separate individuals with their own temperaments, personalities, and needs

6. Made an effort to avoid situations that would cause conflict, but if a conflict did arise were flexible in their attempts to resolve it.

Mothers of Infants Exhibiting Insecure Infant-Mother Attachment

1. Seemed inaccessible and insensitive to their infants

2. Either failed to notice their infants' signals or, if they did notice, often ignored them

3. Responded to their infants in ways that depended heavily on their own moods and activities

4. Showed no respect for their infants' individuality, but rather tried to impose their own will on the babies

5. Became angry and resentful when the babies' behavior was irritating or annoying.

Most people, I think, would predict that problems would arise in the relationship where parents took the latter approach—and here I am including fathers in the discussion.

Based on the behavior just described, we can safely make some assumptions about the expectations of parents whose infants exhibit an insecure infant-mother attachment. For example, we can assume that when they planned to have their baby, they expected their lives to change very little, if at all. When the baby arrived, they were firm and strong-minded and assumed that they would be able to determine when and how long the baby would sleep, when the baby would eat, even when and how the baby would play. They did not expect the infant to have his or her own temperament that no amount of disciplining would change, nor did they have an awareness of babies' developmental stages and how babies are limited in what they can do and learn. These parents no doubt believed that the reason one infant sleeps through the night and feeds on a regular four-hour schedule while another wakes often during the night and feeds erratically and frequently was that the parents of the former infant were firm and consistent and those of the latter were lax.

Here's an example. Sandy and Herb came to see me for a prenatal visit and asked me to help resolve an argument they had been having. The baby was due in six weeks and they were doing some work on their house to get ready. They had a number of valuable glass objects, they told me, which they kept on a low coffee table in the living room. Herb had mentioned that they would have to move these out of reach soon after the baby was born, suggesting that as soon as the baby became mobile and started to crawl, he or she would naturally be attracted to the glass objects.

Sandy was outraged at the idea of moving them. "We'll have them exactly where they are," she argued, "and teach the baby not to touch them. What better opportunity to set boundaries and make the meaning of 'no' perfectly clear?"

I agreed with the father, explaining that it was unrealistic to expect a crawling eight-month-old to learn the kind of self-control Sandy was envisioning. I tried to suggest that their lifestyle would have to change considerably when the baby arrived. Perhaps I shouldn't have been surprised when Sandy and Herb chose another pediatrician.

The parents of the infant with a secure infant-mother attachment realize that the infant is a person with a distinct temperament and unique personality who cannot be molded to fit their idea of the perfect baby and who cannot be rushed through the natural course of development. And because the baby is unique, the parents will discern—even from the very first days after birth—his or her needs, desires, likes, and dislikes by interpreting the baby's signals. The parents will learn to respond when the baby signals hunger, and not insist on a schedule based on convenience. They will put the baby to sleep when he or she seems tired, and not when they want to be free. When the infant is crawling, they will "baby-proof" the house so the baby is free to roam. All this hinges on the understanding that from the very first, the baby is a distinct individual.

Remember Phase 1 of the infant-mother attachment? At this time, the first three months, the baby is sending signals out into an undifferentiated universe—he or she is unable to distinguish among care-givers or perceive distinctions in the environment. The parents respond, thus instilling a sense that the environment is indeed responsive, a place where the baby can feel secure in the expectation that his or her messages will be answered. Parents who attempt to mold the baby to meet their expectations and are *not* responsive to his or her signals are not instilling a sense of security in the infant, but rather anxiety. In this very young baby, such anxiety will be a wordless sensation of fear: "I'm hungry. Will I be fed?" or "I need attention. Will someone come?" Instinctively, this baby will cry a great deal to get his or her needs met.

Again and again, I have emphasized the role of the baby's individual temperament in affecting the infant-parent relationship. In this regard it is important to qualify what I have just said about the anxiety level of a baby whose individual needs are not met. With a baby who is easygoing and has naturally regular eating and sleeping habits, a lack of parental responsiveness may *not* disrupt the relationship. This baby may be so adaptable that even the most minimal or accidental parental responses will do the trick. The problem is in a combination of parents who expect to mold the infant and a tenacious baby with irregular habits and strong desires. As you already know, the same combination of parental expectation and infant behavior is the formula for infant colic syndrome.

In the households of the infant-mother pairs in her sample, Ainsworth studied how the mothers fed their babies and how they responded to their cries. She confirmed that in the majority of pairs in which the mother-infant attachment was classified as secure, the babies were fed on demand. But even more interesting to us is what Ainsworth turned up about crying. The data reveals that when the mothers tended to ignore the crying during the first three months, their babies cried *more* in the last three months of the first year than those infants whose mothers were most responsive to their cries. In other words, Ainsworth's study proved that responding to the infant's cries produced not a baby who cried and "demanded" more, as the "spoiling" theorists had it, but rather one who cried less as time went on. My own studies confirm these findings: Letting babies cry only causes more crying; responding on the assumption that the baby's cries are signals reduces crying.

The key factor, then, to a secure infant-parent attachment? *Responsiveness*—also the key to curing and preventing colic. Ainsworth's work shows that during the first three months, a bond is established and the child learns that the environment is indeed responsive. During this same period, the parent is learning, through observation and experience, precisely *how* to respond. The fact that you are concerned about the extent of your baby's cries and are reading this book to learn their function can only mean that you are actively involved in responding to the cries. In getting to know your baby and learning to interpret his or her cries, and in reading this book as part of that effort, you are doing the very work that is appropriate for the first three months. But it is important to try to prevent or eliminate colic *before* it becomes a serious problem that adversely affects the parent-infant attachment.

AFTER THE FIRST YEAR

Researchers have used Ainsworth's idea of combining strangers with infants in a number of studies to measure the infant-mother attachment in babies a year and a half old and have then followed the children as far as age six to match the level of security to the children's personalities and psychological development. The results have been interesting, if predictable. At eighteen to twenty-four months, babies with a secure infant-mother attachment have more self-comforting skills than insecurely attached infants. They also show more effective imaginative play, which is important to cognitive development. The secure twenty-one-month-olds were found to be more cooperative with their mothers and better behaved. And psychological testing showed that these babies had more self-awareness than the insecurely attached babies, a development important to the learning of independence.

At age two, securely attached children were more independent and more responsible for themselves than the other toddlers. The evidence goes on in the same way all the way up to age six. All the skills that children need to master their world—curiosity, sharing, enthusiasm in play, ego resilience, social interaction, cognitive development—were found to be more strongly developed in children who were securely attached to their mothers than those whose attachment fell into the "insecure" category.

One final note is necessary to qualify this discussion of the infant-parent relationship, and it is a note of caution. Although research examining many cases and analyzing and controlling the influences that affect them can tell us much about a group as a whole, it can tell us very little about the individual person. This means that in every study, there were some infants with a secure infant-mother attachment at one year of age who did not show the greatest accomplishments or highest level of development when tested later on; likewise, there were infants whose attachment fell into the "insecure" category who at one year of age were the stars of their group.

What accounts for these deviations from the predicted norms? Uniqueness is the human being's most consistent quality, and the one many of us treasure most. Many, many elements go into a child's internal makeup. In addition, there is a near infinity of external factors—siblings, the patterns of family life, schools, day care, peer groups, and so on—that affect the child as well. Anything can happen, and anything that *does* happen will have an impact on the baby, as on everyone else in the household. I don't believe that the course of a child's entire development can be determined in the first few days of life. Nor do I believe that a child's development can be determined by what happens in the first *year* of life. Our best goal as parents is to learn as much as we can about babies and about a parent's relationship with them and strive to do the best we can.

GOING EASY ON YOURSELF

Throughout this book, I have emphasized the importance of responding to your baby's cries with accurate responses. But in this chapter full of qualifiers, I want to end with perhaps the most encompassing qualifier of all. It is important to realize that you will not be able to interpret your baby's cries all the time; there will be instances when you will be baffled, when you will simply be unable to determine what your baby needs. And there will be other times when you will be unable to respond as rapidly as you might wish, not because you can't interpret the cries but because circumstances make it impossible.

Please remind yourself at those times that you are doing the best you can, that you love your baby, and that your actions express your love. Individual episodes of frustration and agitation will not permanently harm your baby any more than temporary frustration damages your own well being. More important than particular instances of crying is the general attitude you have toward your infant and his or her cries. Remember that crying is communication and enjoy the process of gradually coming to know your baby in these first exciting, foundation-building months.

References

Ainsworth, M. D. S., M.C. Blehar, E. Waters, and S. Wall. *Patterns of Infant Attachment* (Hillsdale, NJ: Erlbaum, 1978).

Bowlby, John. "The nature of the child's tie to his mother." *International Journal of Psychoanalysis* 39 (1958): 350-373.

Klaus, M., and J. Kennell. *Maternal-Infant Bonding* (St. Louis: C.V. Mosby, 1977).

Daily Diary Page

Name _____

Day/Date _____

a.m.   p.m.   (circle one)

Activity Code

S   =   Sleeping alone (not held)
SH =   Sleeping held
F   =   Feeding
AAH   =   Awake, alone, and happy (in crib, infant
                          seat, swing, etc., but not held)
AAC =   Awake, alone, and crying
AHH =   Awake, held, and happy
AHC =   Awake, held, and crying
(W) =   Being walked
(R) =   Being rocked
B   =   Being bathed
(P) =   Pacifier

Hour	Start Time	Activity	Minutes of Crying
12			
1			
2			
3			
4			
5			
6			
7			
8			
9			
10			
11			

Total minutes crying: [ ]

Daily Diary Page

Name _____

Day/Date _____

a.m.   p.m.   (circle one)

Activity Code

S   =   Sleeping alone (not held)
SH =   Sleeping held
F   =   Feeding
AAH   =   Awake, alone, and happy (in crib, infant
                        seat, swing, etc., but not held)
AAC =   Awake, alone, and crying
AHH =   Awake, held, and happy
AHC =   Awake, held, and crying
(W) =   Being walked
(R) =   Being rocked
B   =   Being bathed
(P) =   Pacifier

Hour	Start Time	Activity	Minutes of Crying
12			
1			
2			
3			
4			
5			
6			
7			
8			
9			
10			
11			

Total minutes crying: [ ]

Daily Diary Page

Name _____

Day/Date _____

a.m.   p.m.   (circle one)

Activity Code

S   =   Sleeping alone (not held)
SH =   Sleeping held
F   =   Feeding
AAH   =   Awake, alone, and happy (in crib, infant
                          seat, swing, etc., but not held)
AAC =   Awake, alone, and crying
AHH =   Awake, held, and happy
AHC =   Awake, held, and crying
(W) =   Being walked
(R) =   Being rocked
B   =   Being bathed
(P) =   Pacifier

Hour	Start Time	Activity	Minutes of Crying
12			
1			
2			
3			
4			
5			
6			
7			
8			
9			
10			
11			

Total minutes crying:

Daily Diary Page

Name _____

Day/Date _____

a.m.   p.m.   (circle one)

Activity Code

S   =   Sleeping alone (not held)
SH   =   Sleeping held
F   =   Feeding
AAH =   Awake, alone, and happy (in crib, infant
                seat, swing, etc., but not held)
AAC =   Awake, alone, and crying
AHH =   Awake, held, and happy
AHC =   Awake, held, and crying
(W) =   Being walked
(R) =   Being rocked
B   =   Being bathed
(P) =   Pacifier

Hour	Start Time	Activity	Minutes of Crying
12			
1			
2			
3			
4			
5			
6			
7			
8			
9			
10			
11			

Total minutes crying: [   ]

Daily Diary Page

Name _____

Day/Date _____

a.m.   p.m.   (circle one)

Activity Code

S   =   Sleeping alone (not held)
SH =   Sleeping held
F   =   Feeding
AAH   =   Awake, alone, and happy (in crib, infant seat, swing, etc., but not held)
AAC   =   Awake, alone, and crying
AHH   =   Awake, held, and happy
AHC   =   Awake, held, and crying
(W) =   Being walked
(R) =   Being rocked
B   =   Being bathed
(P) =   Pacifier

Hour	Start Time	Activity	Minutes of Crying
12			
1			
2			
3			
4			
5			
6			
7			
8			
9			
10			
11			

Total minutes crying:

Daily Diary Page

Name _____

Day/Date _____

a.m.   p.m.   (circle one)

Activity Code

S   =   Sleeping alone (not held)
SH =   Sleeping held
F   =   Feeding
AAH   =   Awake, alone, and happy (in crib, infant
                  seat, swing, etc., but not held)
AAC   =   Awake, alone, and crying
AHH   =   Awake, held, and happy
AHC   =   Awake, held, and crying
(W) =   Being walked
(R) =   Being rocked
B   =   Being bathed
(P) =   Pacifier

Hour	Start Time	Activity	Minutes of Crying
12			
1			
2			
3			
4			
5			
6			
7			
8			
9			
10			
11			

Total minutes crying:

Daily Diary Page

Name _____

Day/Date _____

a.m.   p.m.   (circle one)

Activity Code

S   =   Sleeping alone (not held)
SH =   Sleeping held
F   =   Feeding
AAH   =   Awake, alone, and happy (in crib, infant seat, swing, etc., but not held)
AAC   =   Awake, alone, and crying
AHH   =   Awake, held, and happy
AHC   =   Awake, held, and crying
(W) =   Being walked
(R) =   Being rocked
B   =   Being bathed
(P) =   Pacifier

Hour	Start Time	Activity	Minutes of Crying
12			
1			
2			
3			
4			
5			
6			
7			
8			
9			
10			
11			

Total minutes crying: [   ]

Daily Diary Page

Name _____

Day/Date _____

a.m.   p.m.   (circle one)

Activity Code

S   =   Sleeping alone (not held)
SH =   Sleeping held
F   =   Feeding
AAH   =   Awake, alone, and happy (in crib, infant
                    seat, swing, etc., but not held)
AAC =   Awake, alone, and crying
AHH =   Awake, held, and happy
AHC =   Awake, held, and crying
(W) =   Being walked
(R) =   Being rocked
B   =   Being bathed
(P) =   Pacifier

Hour	Start Time	Activity	Minutes of Crying
12			
1			
2			
3			
4			
5			
6			
7			
8			
9			
10			
11			

Total minutes crying: ☐

Daily Diary Page

Name _____

Day/Date _____

a.m.   p.m.   (circle one)

Activity Code

S   =   Sleeping alone (not held)
SH =   Sleeping held
F   =   Feeding
AAH   =   Awake, alone, and happy (in crib, infant
                 seat, swing, etc., but not held)
AAC   =   Awake, alone, and crying
AHH   =   Awake, held, and happy
AHC   =   Awake, held, and crying
(W) =   Being walked
(R) =   Being rocked
B   =   Being bathed
(P) =   Pacifier

Hour	Start Time	Activity	Minutes of Crying
12			
1			
2			
3			
4			
5			
6			
7			
8			
9			
10			
11			

Total minutes crying:

Daily Diary Page

Name _____

Day/Date _____

a.m.   p.m.   (circle one)

Activity Code

S   =   Sleeping alone (not held)
SH =   Sleeping held
F   =   Feeding
AAH   =   Awake, alone, and happy (in crib, infant
                seat, swing, etc., but not held)
AAC   =   Awake, alone, and crying
AHH   =   Awake, held, and happy
AHC   =   Awake, held, and crying
(W) =   Being walked
(R) =   Being rocked
B   =   Being bathed
(P) =   Pacifier

Hour	Start Time	Activity	Minutes of Crying
12			
1			
2			
3			
4			
5			
6			
7			
8			
9			
10			
11			

Total minutes crying:

Daily Diary Page

Name _____

Day/Date _____

a.m.   p.m.   (circle one)

Activity Code

S   =   Sleeping alone (not held)
SH =   Sleeping held
F   =   Feeding
AAH   =   Awake, alone, and happy (in crib, infant
                         seat, swing, etc., but not held)
AAC =   Awake, alone, and crying
AHH =   Awake, held, and happy
AHC =   Awake, held, and crying
(W) =   Being walked
(R) =   Being rocked
B   =   Being bathed
(P) =   Pacifier

Hour	Start Time	Activity	Minutes of Crying
12			
1			
2			
3			
4			
5			
6			
7			
8			
9			
10			
11			

Total minutes crying:

Daily Diary Page

Name _____

Day/Date _____

a.m.   p.m.   (circle one)

Activity Code

S   =   Sleeping alone (not held)
SH =   Sleeping held
F   =   Feeding
AAH   =   Awake, alone, and happy (in crib, infant
                    seat, swing, etc., but not held)
AAC   =   Awake, alone, and crying
AHH   =   Awake, held, and happy
AHC   =   Awake, held, and crying
(W) =   Being walked
(R) =   Being rocked
B   =   Being bathed
(P) =   Pacifier

Hour	Start Time	Activity	Minutes of Crying
12			
1			
2			
3			
4			
5			
6			
7			
8			
9			
10			
11			

Total minutes crying: [   ]

Daily Diary Page

Name _____

Day/Date _____

a.m.   p.m.   (circle one)

Activity Code

S   =   Sleeping alone (not held)
SH =   Sleeping held
F   =   Feeding
AAH =   Awake, alone, and happy (in crib, infant
                    seat, swing, etc., but not held)
AAC =   Awake, alone, and crying
AHH =   Awake, held, and happy
AHC =   Awake, held, and crying
(W) =   Being walked
(R) =   Being rocked
B   =   Being bathed
(P) =   Pacifier

Hour	Start Time	Activity	Minutes of Crying
12			
1			
2			
3			
4			
5			
6			
7			
8			
9			
10			
11			

Total minutes crying:

Daily Diary Page

Name _____

Day/Date _____

a.m.   p.m.   (circle one)

Activity Code

S   =   Sleeping alone (not held)
SH =   Sleeping held
F   =   Feeding
AAH   =   Awake, alone, and happy (in crib, infant
                              seat, swing, etc., but not held)
AAC   =   Awake, alone, and crying
AHH   =   Awake, held, and happy
AHC   =   Awake, held, and crying
(W) =   Being walked
(R) =   Being rocked
B   =   Being bathed
(P) =   Pacifier

Hour	Start Time	Activity	Minutes of Crying
12			
1			
2			
3			
4			
5			
6			
7			
8			
9			
10			
11			

Total minutes crying:

Daily Diary Page

Name _____

Day/Date _____

a.m.   p.m.   (circle one)

Activity Code

S   =   Sleeping alone (not held)
SH =   Sleeping held
F   =   Feeding
AAH   =   Awake, alone, and happy (in crib, infant
                            seat, swing, etc., but not held)
AAC =   Awake, alone, and crying
AHH =   Awake, held, and happy
AHC =   Awake, held, and crying
(W) =   Being walked
(R) =   Being rocked
B   =   Being bathed
(P) =   Pacifier

Hour	Start Time	Activity	Minutes of Crying
12			
1			
2			
3			
4			
5			
6			
7			
8			
9			
10			
11			

Total minutes crying:

Daily Diary Page

Name _____

Day/Date _____

a.m.   p.m.   (circle one)

Activity Code

S   =   Sleeping alone (not held)
SH =   Sleeping held
F   =   Feeding
AAH   =   Awake, alone, and happy (in crib, infant
                    seat, swing, etc., but not held)
AAC   =   Awake, alone, and crying
AHH   =   Awake, held, and happy
AHC   =   Awake, held, and crying
(W) =   Being walked
(R) =   Being rocked
B   =   Being bathed
(P) =   Pacifier

Hour	Start Time	Activity	Minutes of Crying
12			
1			
2			
3			
4			
5			
6			
7			
8			
9			
10			
11			

Total minutes crying:

Index

ABOUT THE AUTHOR

A graduate of the University of Wisconsin and Albert Einstein College of Medicine, Dr. Taubman is affiliated with the Children's Hospital of Philadelphia's Division of Gastroenterology and Nutrition, and is a Clinical Associate Professor in the Department of Pediatrics, Division of Gastroenterology and Nutrition, at the University of Pennsylvania's  School of Medicine. He also is in private practice in Cherry Hill, New Jersey. His colic studies have been published in *Pediatrics* as well as featured in other national publications.

He received the American Academy of Pediatrics Practitioners Research Award and has written sections in several textbooks on the treatment of colic.